Resourc

Books, Recordings, Coachii

Whenever I feel l
read a couple of pages and feel inspired to write again.
Anna Blagoslavova – Moscow, Russia

A highly recommended guide from one of the most creative people around.
William C. Reichard – author of "Evertime"

Mark David Gerson will make your book-writing dreams
a reality. I know. He did it for me!
Karen Helene Walker – author of "The Wishing Steps"

Without Mark David's inspiration, example and encouragement, I might
never have had the courage to publish my book.
Nancy Pogue LaTurner – author of "Voluntary Nomads"

Coaching with Mark David Gerson: Best investment ever!
Christine Farris – Denver, CO

I owe so much to Mark David! He helped me believe in myself enough
to write the book that got two wrongful murder convictions overturned.
Estelle Blackburn – author of "Broken Lives"

Memoirs

Acts of Surrender: A Writer's Memoir
Pilgrimage: A Fool's Journey
Dialogues with the Divine: Encounters with My Wisest Self

A dynamic read for the creative spirit within each of us.
Positive inspiration at its best.
Hank Bruce – author of "Peace Beyond All Fear: A Tribute to
John Denver's Vision"

A book that has the power to awaken, empower and inspire
anyone who reads it.
Melissa Shawn – Austin, Texas

Read it, love it, pass it on and share Mark David's gift
with someone you love.
Paola Rizzato – Heysham, UK

Self-Help & Personal Growth

*The Way of the Fool, The Way of the Imperfect Fool,
The Book of Messages*

It will transform your life!
REV. BRENDALYN BATCHELOR – UNITY SANTA FE

Simple but powerful!
DAVE KERPEN – AUTHOR OF "THE ART OF PEOPLE"

A book that changes everything that's holding you back!
TED WIGA – SAN FRANCISCO, CA

The Legend of Q'ntana

*The MoonQuest, The StarQuest, The SunQuest,
The Bard of Bryn Doon*
(Soon to Be a Series of Epic Fantasy Films)

An exceptional, timeless novel.
"MINDQUEST REVIEW OF BOOKS"

You will love this book!
AMY ROBBINS-WILSON – AUTHOR, SINGER/SONGWRITER

Magic, music and universal truths masterfully woven into a gripping tale.
BETTY DRAVIS, AUTHOR OF "1106 GRAND BOULEVARD"

Leaves you turning every single page, hungry for more!
DAVID MICHAEL – AUTHOR OF "THE UNITED SERIES"

The Sara Stories

Sara's Year, After Sara's Year, The Emmeline Papers

Honest and heartfelt. Brilliant!
JOAN CERIO – HOST OF RADIO'S "EARTH ENERGY FORECAST"

Thrilling...bittersweet...triumphant!
DAN STONE – AUTHOR OF "ICE ON FIRE"

A classic in the making!
D'ARCY MAYO – MITTAGONG, AUSTRALIA

ORGANIC SCREENWRITING

Writing for Film, Naturally

Mark David Gerson

Organic Screenwriting: Writing for Film, Naturally

First Edition 2014. Second Edition 2019.

Published by MDG Media International
2370 W. State Route 89a
Suite 11-210
Sedona, AZ 86336
www.mdgmediainternational.com

ISBN: 978-1-950189-07-6

Cover Photograph: Kathleen Messmer
www.kathleenmessmer.com

Author Photograph: Kevin Truong
www.kevintruong.com

Coming Soon to a Theater Near You: Epic Motion Pictures from
Mark David Gerson's Screenplay Adaptations of His Fantasy Novels!

More resources for writers
www.books4writers.com

More information on the author
www.markdavidgerson.com

NEIL GAIMAN (SCREENWRITER & HUGO AWARD-WINNING NOVELIST)

Just to do it. Put one word after the other until you've made something that didn't exist before.

This book is dedicated to the unsung screenwriters whose filmed stories have touched and inspired so many, including me, over the decades. The stars and directors may get all the fame and celebrity, but without your imagination, passion and commitment, there would be neither stars nor directors for us to celebrate. And there would be no movies. Thank you!

And to all those who find externally imposed structures suffocating and anti-creative: This book is for you.

Contents

Organic Screenwriting: The Remake

STEVEN SPIELBERG (OSCAR-WINNING PRODUCER/
DIRECTOR)

I don't dream at night, I dream all day; I dream
for a living.

JOHN CASSAVETES (OSCAR-NOMINATED DIRECTOR/
SCREENWRITER)

If you don't put your innermost thoughts on the
screen, then you are looking down on not only your
audience but on the people you work with.

A writer never knows, when rereading work that's more than a couple of years old, whether or not it still "fits." After all, authors grow and evolve but their books hover in a single moment in time, photographs snapped the moment the final period drops on their final draft.

So I approached the first edition of *Organic Screenwriting* with a certain amount of trepidation, as well as with two questions:

- If the manuscript were new, would I publish it as eagerly today as I did five years ago?

- Could a "remake" improve on the original?

My answer to the first question, I was relieved to discover as I began to reread the book, was an unqualified *yes*. As for the second question, it didn't take me long to come up with ways both subtle and dramatic to take my five-year-old "photograph" and make it current. So that, too, was a *yes*.

The result is this new, expanded edition — this "remake," as it were.

What has changed? I have incorporated new exercises and meditations, expanded the section on how to edit your screenplay and reorganized some of the existing material for clarity and better flow. I even caught a few of the typos that slipped into the original edition, although I can't promise that new ones haven't weaseled their way into this one!

With these major additions and a host of minor ones, this *Organic Screenwriting* "remake" is nearly fifteen percent longer than the original and, I hope, at least fifteen percent more effective! May it inspire you to unleash your creative potential and may it guide you to transform your vision, naturally and organically, into form. And may the resulting screenplay find its way not only onto movie screens around the world, but into the hearts of moviegoers everywhere!

Mark David Gerson
Portland, Oregon
April 2019

Fade In

ALAN J. PAKULA (OSCAR-NOMINATED SCREENWRITER OF
"SOPHIE'S CHOICE")

The very nature of being a creative person is
being, in some way, eccentric.

CLAUDE-MICHEL SCHÖNBERG (OSCAR-NOMINATED
COMPOSER & TONY AWARD-WINNING WRITER/COMPOSER
OF "LES MISERABLES")

I never decided to be a composer. The music
decided for me.

It's May 2006 and I'm on I-40 driving west from Wisconsin to New Mexico when my cellphone rings.

"What's happening with *The MoonQuest*?" a friend asks me. *The MoonQuest* is my first novel, and my friend is wondering whether my agent has sold it yet.

"Nothing," I reply unhappily. I tell her that the agent and I have parted ways and that *The MoonQuest* is in limbo.

"Write it as a screenplay," my friend suggests, not for the first time.

Even when I was working on the novel, I envisioned *The MoonQuest* as a movie, secretly fantasizing about Steven Spielberg as director. But I never intended to write the screenplay myself. What did I know about screenwriting?

Through the rest of my drive to Santa Fe, I can't get the idea of a *MoonQuest* screenplay out of my head. It makes no sense for me to write it, but I will.

My first stop when I get into town is Borders Books: If I'm to write a film script, I will need help, lots of it. I scour the bookstore's shelves, eliminate most candidates as too structured and rule-bound, settle into the cafe and begin to read.

When I leave Borders a few hours later, I am even more doubtful that traditional approaches to the craft will work for me. Writing for film still feels discouragingly architectural and I'm uncertain where to turn.

You know everything you need to know, an inner voice whispers as I start up the car.

I'm not convinced. Screenplays are technical, demanding creatures. Where do I begin? How do I begin? Then I laugh. Those were my protagonist's same questions in the opening pages of *The MoonQuest* book. If Na'an and M'nor helped Toshar, and me, a decade ago on the first draft of the novel, I will have to trust them to help me again on this film version of the story.

As I did with the book, I get out of my own way and listen. I try not to think about structure, beats or plot points and do my best to let the story tell me how to make it work for the screen. As with all my writing, it is an intuitive process and comes with many moments of doubt, distrust and self-judgment. Yet by summer's end, I have completed two drafts.

Today, several years and many drafts later, I have a film deal — not only for *The MoonQuest* but for its sequels in what is now called *The Legend of Q'ntana*.

I share this story because it speaks to the core of what I believe, not only about screenwriting but about writing, and that's that creativity is an organic process that relies more on discernment than rules, more on intuition than outlines, more on passion than structure. It's a free-flowing, in-the-moment experience that urges us to turn our backs on cookie-cutter formulas and paint-by-numbers canvasses. It's a realm where Story is king and Muse is both chancellor and court jester. It's a journey where we sit, wide-eyed, in a darkened theater and watch, awe-struck, as our screenplay reveals itself to us on the flickering screen.

I found little of this expressed in the screenwriting books I browsed through all those years ago, even though many contained valid and valuable information.

"If there's a book you really want to read, but it hasn't been written yet," author Toni Morrison once said, "then you must write it." *Organic Screenwriting* is for me that book.

In the pages ahead, I won't be covering format, structure or other technical aspects of the craft. Nor will I explain how to write a logline, how best to pitch your finished script or how to break into Hollywood. Scores of books already do that.

Instead, I will offer you something no other screenwriting book does: a radical approach to storytelling that will inspire and empower you to birth those screenplays that long to find expression through you onto page and screen — both the stories you think you know and those that have until now hidden themselves from your conscious mind. As well, I will guide you from first to final draft through a revision process that is both effective and innovative. And I will do this all without ignoring the sometimes harsh realities of the filmmaking world.

Whether you are a seasoned screenwriter or just starting out, I guarantee that *Organic Screenwriting* will not only revolutionize your approach to the craft, but free your stories to surge from you more effortlessly than you could ever have imagined.

If the popcorn's ready (it doesn't have to be organic, but don't forget the butter!), turn the page and let's get started.

Scene 1.
Getting Started

EMIR KUSTURICA (CÉSAR AWARD-WINNING WRITER/
DIRECTOR OF "ZIVOT JE CUDO")

I know that a scene is good when I feel my heart
beat faster…

PATRICIA ROUTLEDGE (ACTOR & THREE-TIME BAFTA
NOMINEE)

I'll give you a tip — it's risk. Once you're
willing to risk everything, you can accomplish
anything.

Going Organic

A few weeks after my experience at Santa Fe's downtown Borders, I found myself sitting in an Albuquerque cafe absentmindedly thumbing through the *Alibi*, the city's alternative weekly. Suddenly, an ad caught my eye: The Screenwriting Conference in Santa Fe, a major industry confab, was scheduled to start in a few days. Awed by the synchronicity, I registered on the spot.

Although the event failed to furnish me with what I had hoped to find on Borders' shelves, it did energize me. I left Santa Fe more determined than ever to complete my *MoonQuest* script, despite the slight-seeming odds of getting it produced. It didn't matter. It couldn't matter. As with *The MoonQuest* book a decade earlier, it was something I had to write.

When, three years later, I was invited to join the 2009 conference's faculty, I was initially stumped. What would I teach? The answer soon became clear: I would teach what I had learned from writing *The MoonQuest*. I would teach what I hadn't found among Borders' screenwriting books. I would teach the same precepts I had taught other writers over the years, but I would adapt it to the distinctive needs of screenwriters. And I would call the concept "organic screenwriting."

Without knowing it, I was birthing this book.

Why "organic" screenwriting? Because writing for film doesn't have to feel like an engineered exercise in story-*building*. Rather, it can be a story-*freeing* adventure not unlike those undertaken by explorers of old: a journey of discovery and rediscovery that retains all the magic, wonder, spontaneity and awe of childhood and make-believe.

That's what *Organic Screenwriting* is about — not only in its content but in its presentation. As I will point out frequently in the pages ahead, there are no rules when it comes to creativity. As such, there can be no rules when it comes to using this book, which is all about accessing your creativity in the most natural ways possible. Read *Organic Screenwriting* straight through if that's your inclination. Or leap randomly from chapter to chapter as your intuition dictates.

My only urging is that, after this section, your next stop be "On Screen with the Muse Stream" (Scene 2), whose chapters lay the foundation upon which the rest of *Organic Screenwriting* is built. I also encourage you to spend some time with the exercises and guided meditations scattered through the book, all of which are designed to not only enrich your screenplays and make your characters and dialogue more dynamic, but to make your screenwriting experience more free-flowing and, well, organic.

So what are you waiting for? The house lights are dimming. It's time for the show to begin!

Guided Meditations

Whenever I facilitate a screenwriting workshop or seminar, I nearly always incorporate a guided journey as part of the experience. It's an opportunity for writers to, in a sense, lose their mind and find their heart — the heart of a particular project and the heart of their creative process. For that reason, I have included eight guided meditations in *Organic Screenwriting*.

Among their other purposes, these immersive experiences are designed to help you...

- Connect with the spirit and essence of your story, even if you're not yet sure what that story is.

- Create compelling characters and place them in unforgettable settings.

- Free yourself from harsh self-judgment and tame your inner critic.

- Stay true to your vision for your screenplay, as well as to your vision for yourself as a screenwriter.

- Affirm your creative power.

HOW TO USE A GUIDED MEDITATION

- Record it yourself for playback.

- Have a friend read it to you, then return the favor.

- Get into a quiet place/inner space, set your music player for five to forty-five minutes of contemplative music or nature sounds (depending on the length of the exercise) and read the meditation slowly and receptively, following its directions and suggestions.

For a more professionally guided approach, I have recorded the five following meditations (along with an additional five not included in this book) on my album *The Voice of the Muse Companion: Guided Meditations for Writers.*

- "Let Judgment Go" (Scene 3: "Thirteen Creativity-Killing Myths About Screenwriting")
- "Your Ocean of Stories" (Scene 5: "Screenplay Craft: Getting Inspired")
- "Vision Quest" (Scene 9: "Cine-Vision")
- "Taming Your Critic" (Scene 10: "Taming Your Inner Film Critic")
- "You Are a Writer" ("Fade Out")

HOW TO ACCESS THE RECORDED MEDITATIONS

- Stream "Let Judgment Go," "Your Ocean of Stories," "Taming Your Critic" and "You Are a Writer" for free as a subscriber to Apple Music, YouTube Music or Amazon's Music Unlimited, or download those individual tracks from Amazon or Apple Music.
- Experience a video version of "You Are a Writer" on my YouTube channel, www.youtube.com/markdavidgerson.
- "Vision Quest" is available only on *The Voice of the Muse Companion* album, not as a stand-alone track. Download the album from my website or from Apple Music, Amazon or CD Baby.

Scene 2.
On Screen with the Muse Stream

PETER HANSON (SCREENWRITER, DIRECTOR & PRODUCER)

I let the story tell itself.

GUILLERMO ARRIAGA (OSCAR-NOMINATED SCREENWRITER OF "PAN'S LABYRINTH")

I don't research, I don't write any kind of outline, I don't try to have any kind of structure. I don't have any character development beforehand. I just try to sit down and write.

What's a Muse Stream?

Although I had written *The MoonQuest* novel on what I call the "Muse Stream," I wasn't convinced, when I began my film adaptation, that this technique would work as effectively with a screenplay.

I was wrong.

As I have discovered over the years, there is no medium or genre that the Muse Stream cannot facilitate and catalyze. Despite its non-prose structure and strict format requirements, a screenplay is no less about igniting imagination and freeing up flow than any other creative enterprise. And imagination and flow is what the Muse Stream is all about.

So what is a Muse Stream? It's an unstructured, uncensored, right-brain outpouring onto the page. If you have ever written morning pages or experienced free writing, stream-of-consciousness writing or automatic writing, then you have already dipped your toes into the limpid waters of the Muse Stream. But while those other techniques are prescribed primarily as personal-growth exercises or to prime your creative pump, the Muse Stream is more than that. Much more.

If you dive into it and surrender unconditionally to its current, the Muse Stream will write the first draft of your screenplay for you. It's that simple.

Here's how it works: Type FADE IN and start writing what you know of your story, even if it's nothing at all. Once you begin, *don't stop*.

- Don't stop to correct spelling punctuation or grammar as you write. There is a time for editing, revising and correcting. That time is *not* in the midst of a rush of creativity.

- Don't stop to grope for the word that's on the tip of your tongue or to search for synonyms. Just leave a blank space or type *xxxx* and keep going.

- Don't stop to read over what you have already written.

- Don't stop moving forward with your draft to rewrite what you've already committed to the page.

- Don't stop to worry about consistency or redundancy — be it in characters, dialogue or settings. You will have ample opportunity to deal with all of those in future drafts.

- Don't stop to consult index cards or outlines. (See Myth #3 in "Thirteen Creativity-Killing Myths About Screenwriting")

- Don't stop to obsess over your screenplay's format. Formatting is a finicky left-brain activity that has no place in the freely flowing waters of your Muse Stream. If you are unsure how to format some aspect of your screenplay, jot down a quick reminder to look into it later and continue with your story.

- Don't stop to structure your script. Don't stop to analyze beats or plot points.

- Don't stop to count the number of lines in your action paragraphs.

- Don't stop to worry about scene breaks.

- Don't stop to monitor your page count.

- Don't stop to research. Insert a brief note about what's needed, set aside separate time for research and write on.

Write without stopping, for *any* reason, and the Muse Stream will carry you all the way from FADE IN to FADE OUT — easily, naturally and spontaneously.

You're skeptical. I know you are. Sure, I hear you say, the Muse Stream might work on prose, even on poetry. But on a screenplay, with all its quirks and strictures? It can't be done.

It can.

I have written all the screenplays in my *Legend of Q'ntana* fantasy series on the Muse Stream. And even though I had drafts of *The MoonQuest* and *StarQuest* novels to guide me through those first two scripts, I knew nothing about *The SunQuest* plot when I began; I wrote it as an original screenplay.

Here's why the Muse Stream works: For the most part, we think with the logical, controlling, analytical side of our brain and write with the creative, imaginative, analogical side of our brain. And for the most part, when we do the former, we stunt the latter. When we stop to edit, research, fuss with format or engage our "thinking" mind in any way, we also give voice to judgment, criticism and not-good-enoughs — to that inner fault-finder determined to control a creative process that by its very nature is uncontrollable.

The Muse Stream, on the other hand, is the free-flowing river of creative output that we all aspire to, a river that will *always* transport us to realms beyond the limits of our conscious plotting, outlining and imaginings — if we let it.

The Muse Stream is also the place where writer's block not only does not exist but cannot exist, because it's the place where judgment, low self-esteem and uncertainty — primary causes of writer's block — cannot survive.

When we allow ourselves to give ourselves to it, it's the place where the words of our screenplay tumble unhindered onto the page as swiftly as the waters of a stream tumble down their channel.

Still, you're sure to experience moments when it seems as though a giant boulder is damming up your Muse Stream flow. It happens to all of us. That's why I wrote the next chapter. But before we go there, let me answer the question I get asked most often about writing screenplays on the Muse Stream: "If I write without stopping or thinking, won't my screenplay lack structure and pacing? Won't it be riddled with repetition and inconsistencies? Won't it be a muddled, chaotic mess?"

Probably. But we're talking about first drafts here, and first drafts aren't final drafts. First drafts are journeys of exploration and discovery. First drafts are where your story reveals itself to you. First drafts are where you learn who your characters are. It's okay for your first draft to be a muddled, chaotic mess.

Here's the thing: By writing your first draft on the Muse Stream, you give your story and its characters the freedom to blossom that a more structured and controlled process can never provide. You move past the confines of your conscious imagination and into the infinite realms of storytelling that only your unconscious mind can access. It's in later drafts — as many as it takes — where you can apply the structural and other tools that will help you produce a polished final draft. We'll explore some of those tools when we get to "The Edit Suite" (Scene II).

Read more about the Muse Stream in my book "The Voice of the Muse: Answering the Call to Write."

Navigating the Muse Stream When You Feel Stuck

There are countless reasons why you might find yourself stranded on a shoal in the midst of your Muse Stream. You might be...

- Approaching or in the midst of an emotionally or technically challenging scene
- Trying to write dialogue that is counter to the true nature of a character
- Feeling overwhelmed by the scolding harangue of your inner critic
- Feeling shut down by rejection or negative feedback
- Analyzing or over-thinking the part of the story that is causing you problems
- Feeling held up by a need for additional research
- Breaking faith with the basic "keep writing" principle of the Muse Stream

If you get stuck — it happens — consider one of these thirteen surefire techniques for reigniting your creative fire and restoring the Muse Stream flow of your story and screenplay.

1. WRITE ANYTHING

It doesn't matter what you write. The act of writing *anything* will nearly always dissolve all blocks, barriers and boulders and reestablish an easy stream of words. When the words won't come, try these simple tips for tricking your mind into relinquishing control of the creative process to your Muse.

- **Repetition.** Repeat the last word or sentence you wrote — over and over until the flow returns. Or repeat the first sentence of the previous piece of dialogue or paragraph of action. Or repeat the first word or sentence of your day's writing. Repeat *anything* to keep your fingers moving across your keyboard.

- **Free Association.** Start with the final word of the last sentence you felt able to write and let that word trigger another word — whatever word leaps to mind, however silly. Let that word trigger the next, the next and so on.

- **Jabberwocky.** A little nonsense can go a long way toward freeing up your creativity when you are feeling stuck. "Jabberwocky" is the nonsense poem that Alice discovers in *Through the Looking Glass*. When English words refuse to come, let Lewis Carroll be your guide and make up your own, stringing them together into sentences and paragraphs of silliness.

In each of the above scenarios, keep throwing words onto the screen until the natural flow of your screenplay starts up again, and it will. You can discard what doesn't belong when you get to your next draft.

2. BREATHE

If you're stuck in your writing, you are probably stuck in your breath. Has your breathing become shallow? Pause for a moment and take a deep breath in, hold it for a few counts, then let it go. All of it. Do it again, breathing more deeply. This time, write "I am breathing in" as you inhale and "I am breathing out" as you exhale. Continue writing your breath until you relax back into the Muse Stream.

The key here, as in the previous tip, is to continue writing without stopping. Any way you are able do that will always revive an effortless flow of words.

3. GO PROSE

It's easy to get slowed down — or stopped — by screenwriting's rigid format requirements. When that happens, leave screenplay format behind and continue your storytelling as an unformatted prose narrative. You can convert the scene or scenes back into script form once you have regained the thread of your story or at the start of your next writing session. Or you can leave it until your next draft.

4. CHANGE WRITING TOOLS

Do you normally write on your computer? Get a screenwriting app for your tablet or smartphone and go mobile. Where possible, use a cloud-linked version of the same app to ease the transition between devices.

Maybe it's time to set electronics aside for a bit and instead pick up paper and pen. When we associate our computer (or tablet or phone) with work and the work isn't going well, the accompanying pressure can dam up our creative output. Relieve that pressure and reopen the floodgates.

5. CHANGE VENUES

Some days, a desk, home office or other regular workspace can feel as inhibiting as our electronics did in #4. If your writing device is portable, move to a different room or to a park, library or cafe. If not, change tools as well as venues, and get out that pen and paper.

6. CHANGE LANGUAGES

If English isn't your native language and you find yourself struggling with your script, return to your first language for the day. It will boost your confidence and get your Muse Stream going again. Translate the scene or scenes back into English later, or leave it until your next draft.

7. RETURN TO CENTER

Novelist Anne Tyler has written that when she hits what she calls a "real block," it's "usually because I've taken a wrong turn — said something false or made a character do what he doesn't want to do."

Are you trying to control the world and characters of your screenplay instead of surrendering to their superior wisdom? As I will repeat often through these pages, your story and script are smarter than you are; defying them will always slow you down. Take a break to explore where you have refused to trust your characters and their story.

8. CHANGE FOCUS

Move on to another scene or sequence. Return to this one in an hour, in a day or in a few days — whenever you feel ready or after you have carried out the necessary research, if a research-deficit is what has stopped you. If it's an emotionally challenging segment that is holding you back, perhaps it's time to...

9. WALK AWAY

Sometimes, the best thing to do is to walk away from your screenplay for a spell. Take a break — to research, if that feels right, or to work on a different script or in a different medium.

Or do something unrelated to writing. Go for a stroll or take a bath. Read a book or watch a movie for pleasure. Go for a run or a bike ride. Go to the gym or to a yoga class. Go to a museum or an art gallery. Or go to a concert or theater performance.

If you have other expressive pursuits, engage in an unrelated Muse-like pastime: drawing, photography, singing, furniture-making, cooking...or whatever will keep your creative momentum alive until it's the right time to return to your screenplay.

10. JOURNAL

Use the Muse Stream as a journaling tool to explore why you are feeling stuck. Let whatever emerges guide you back to your screenplay and back into the flow.

11. RECONNECT WITH YOUR VISION

Whether or not we are conscious of it at the time, there is always an "inciting vision" that prompts us to start telling our story...a creative spark that ignites our passion to write a particular screenplay.

Have you lost sight of that vision? Has that creative spark dimmed or extinguished? If so, it can be hard to keep writing. It can be hard to want to keep writing.

In "Cine-Vision" (Scene 9) you will have an opportunity to craft a "vision statement" for your screenplay, a sort of mission statement that expresses your reasons for wanting to tell a story, that puts your passion into words. If you're feeling stuck and nothing else is working, it's time to revisit that vision statement — either to reconnect with your original passion and reignite it or to revise your vision statement to better reflect how you now view the project.

If you are already in mid-screenplay and have yet to draft a vision statement, skip ahead to "Cine-Vision" and do it now — even if you are not currently stuck. Your vision statement will always help you to stay aligned with the true heart of your work, not only in this first draft but all the way to your final draft and beyond.

12. ENGAGE WITH THE SPIRIT AND ESSENCE
OF YOUR STORY

Use the "Spirit of Your Story, the Essence of Your Screenplay" meditation in "Screenplay Craft: Getting Inspired" (Scene 5) to "listen" to what
your screenplay has to tell you.

13. TAME YOUR INNER CRITIC

Use the meditation in "Taming Your Inner Film Critic " (Scene 10) to get
to the heart of your stuckness.

Discover many more techniques to help you get unstuck in my book "Writer's
Block Unblocked: Seven Surefire Ways to Free Up Your Writing and Creative
Flow."

Scene 3.
Thirteen Creativity-Killing Myths About Screenwriting

PEDRO ALMODÒVAR (OSCAR-WINNING WRITER/DIRECTOR OF "HABLE CON ELLA")

I know hundreds of examples proving that one can make a good film by breaking all the rules.

NEIL SIMON (FOUR-TIME OSCAR NOMINEE & GOLDEN GLOBE WINNER FOR "THE GOODBYE GIRL")

I really don't understand the writing process. It's all so instinctive with me. I really don't know what the next line is going to be. One just sits there and it comes.

Perhaps more than any other creative pursuit, writing for film is steeped in absolutist dogma and orthodoxy, with too many books, courses and workshops built around an overwhelming catalogue of "don'ts" and "musts" that screenwriters are warned to ignore at their peril. Most of these are myths that do little other than stunt creativity, stifle storytelling and transform screenwriting from an art and a craft into a manufacturing process.

In the following pages, I debunk thirteen of the most outrageous of those myths.

The Myths

MYTH #1

"Screenwriting is all about rules: I have to follow the rules."

MYTH #1 DEBUNKED!

Creativity has nothing to do with rules. Not now. Not ever.

MYTH #2

"Without discipline, I will never achieve anything."

MYTH #2 DEBUNKED!

Conventional discipline can be punishing and counter-creative.

MYTH #3

"Without an outline (and without index cards), I will never write a coherent script."

MYTH #3 DEBUNKED!

Outlines are overrated and can stifle the free flow of your creativity.

MYTH #4

"If I don't control my story and its characters, I will never write a coherent script."

MYTH #4 DEBUNKED!

Control is a creativity-stifling illusion.

MYTH #5

"I can't start writing if I don't know how my screenplay begins…and ends."

MYTH #5 DEBUNKED!

Your story will guide you, if you let it.

MYTH #6

"I must know everything about my characters before starting."

MYTH #6 DEBUNKED!

Your characters will reveal themselves to you as you write, if you let them.

MYTH #7

"I must write my screenplay in story order."

MYTH #7 DEBUNKED!

Your story will find its own sequence, if you let it.

MYTH #8

"Master dialogue and I will master screenwriting."

MYTH #8 DEBUNKED!

There's more to accomplished screenwriting than dialogue.

MYTH #9

"My screenplay is only a blueprint for the final film: Evocative writing doesn't matter."

MYTH #9 DEBUNKED!

Evocative writing matters.

MYTH #10

"Three-act structure matters: I have to map out my acts."

MYTH #10 DEBUNKED!

All that matters is your story.

MYTH #11

"Screenplay format matters: I have to master proper format before I can start writing."

MYTH #11 DEBUNKED!

Format matters in your screen*play,* not in your screen*writing.*

MYTH #12

"Market trends matter: I have to write what's selling now."

MYTH #12 DEBUNKED!

The market is fickle: Today's trends are irrelevant.

MYTH #13

"I'm not good enough or creative enough to write this story."

MYTH #13 DEBUNKED!

You are good enough and creative enough to write *your* story.

Myth #1: "Screenwriting Is All About Rules. I Have to Follow the Rules"

There are many myths about screenwriting. This, however, is the most widespread and egregious. I will have more to say about rules in "12½ 'Rules' for Writing Your Screenplay" (Scene 4), but for now let me ask you this: How can any creative activity be bound by unyielding commandments? How can any imaginative pursuit be tied to "the way it has always been done"? What is creativity if it's not about breaking new ground and breaking old rules?

Write the story that wants to be written by you, that has chosen you to write it. Write it the way you feel called to write it, the way the story itself would have you write it, not the way you think you should and not the way others tell you that you must. You're a storyteller, not an engineer.

MYTH #1 DEBUNKED!

Creativity has nothing to do with rules.
Not now. Not ever.

Myth #2: "Without Discipline, I Will Never Achieve Anything"

The primary definition for the word "discipline" in *The Oxford English Dictionary* is "the practice of training people to obey rules or a code of behavior, using punishment to correct disobedience." Need I say more?

As a matter of fact, I do — about the word's origins, which are from the Middle English, meaning "mortification by scourging oneself."

Words like "punishment," "disobedience," "mortification" and "scourging" have no place in any discussion about creativity.

MYTH #2 DEBUNKED!
Conventional Discipline Can Be Punishing and Counter-Creative

The problem is that most books on screenwriting insist that success comes only with discipline, a discipline they define, *Oxford*-like, as an ironclad routine that churns out a certain number of words or scenes per day, generally produced during the same time period each day.

My view of discipline is vastly different. As I see it, there are two types a screenwriter can adopt: conventional or "hard" discipline, or what I call "creative" discipline.

Hard discipline, as *The Oxford Dictionary* suggests, is punishing and rule-bound, threatening creative catastrophe should you stray from a strict, butt-in-the-chair routine. Hard discipline is disempowering and mistrustful because it suggests that you lack the commitment to write and the discernment to know when to write. Hard discipline makes it easy to feel shamed, less-than and blocked.

Creative discipline is different. It's not about iron-fisted control. It is not about forcing a creative vision that is boundless in nature to hew to the constraints of a controlling mind or to be constricted by a conventional wisdom that is generally more conventional than it is wise. It's about discipleship. It's about you becoming a disciple — to your passion, to your Muse, to your story.

Creative discipline is about discernment and intuition. Creative discipline is about passion and commitment. Creative discipline knows no hard-and-fast rules, times or goals. Creative discipline is fluid and in-the-moment. Creative discipline places your Muse and story in the driver's seat of your creative enterprise.

"Wait!" I hear you exclaim. "If I don't sit down to my screenplay at the same time every day, how will my Muse know to when show up and start driving?"

That's easy. Your Muse is always present, always available and always ready to get behind the wheel. Can you trust that?

Can you trust that when you sit down to write, whenever you sit down, your Muse will be there for you? Can you trust that all you hear (not all you fear), including that it is either time to write or time to stop, is true? Can you trust that all the words of all the scenes that flow through you on a given day, be they two or two thousand, are the right ones for that day?

Trust is a practice. Practice listening to what's inside you — to the voice of your Muse, to the voice of your passion, to the voice of your screenplay, which is the voice of your intuition and discernment — not to the judgmental, fear-based voices clamoring in your head.

What if you have no passion for the screenplay you're writing? Then you're writing the wrong screenplay.

Write what impassions, electrifies and enlivens you. Write the stories you *must* write. Commit to those stories with all your heart and you will never lack the discipline to get them onto the page.

RHYTHMS AND ROUTINES

Human beings like routine. We like breakfast at a certain hour and a certain kind of bread or pastry with our particular blend or style of coffee or tea. We visit the same websites, interact with the same people on social media, take the same route to work or school, shop at the same stores, and walk the dog along the same streets. Even as parts of us yearn for the unpredictability of adventure, other parts of us crave the control of predictability.

As writers, we are no different. We often prefer our work to follow established patterns and rhythms: working in a certain place, writing at a certain time, setting a certain daily goal, having a certain kind of music playing, drinking our tea or coffee from a certain cup or mug.

There's nothing wrong with routine. It can help free our mind from peripheral decision-making so that we can focus on our screenplay. The problem arises when we are so married to the routine that it becomes more important than the writing, when the routine becomes a rut.

Just like screenplay structure and format, our writing routines exist to serve our story, not the other way around.

Seek out the rhythms and routines that work for you today, the rhythms and routines that support and foster your creative process and creative output. Find them, celebrate them and surrender to them. But be open to changing them. What worked for you yesterday may not work today...or ever again.

Be in the moment with your work flow, just as you are with your word flow.

ASK YOURSELF THESE QUESTIONS

- Do my current writing rhythms and routines support and foster my creative output, or have I fallen into a rut?

- What can I shift — subtly or dramatically — to be in a better rhythm with my work flow and word flow? (Even if you're not feeling stuck, consider shaking up your existing routine every now and again by changing your writing time, writing place, writing goals and/or writing tools. Revisit techniques #4 and #5 in "Navigating the Muse Stream When You Feel Stuck," Scene 2).

TRY THIS

What can you do to break the regular patterns that are keeping you rutted in routine in your non-writing life? Shake those up and watch the effects spill over into your screenwriting day.

If you commute regularly to work, alter your route or mode of transport or both. Is there someplace you regularly shop? Shop somewhere else instead, maybe in a different part of town. Do you have a regular coffee hangout? Try somewhere new, maybe in a neighborhood you don't know, and change your regular drink for something you've never tried before.

What else can you do today to break those regular patterns that are keeping you rutted in routine? Whatever it is, do it. Today. Start now!

Myth #3: "Without an Outline (and without Index Cards), I Will Never Write a Coherent Script"

According to orthodox screenwriting dictates, you must never write a single word of your screenplay until you have prepared a comprehensive, scene-by-scene outline and filled out a stack of index cards to go with it. Launching into a screenplay without these necessary tools, this school of screenwriting insists, sets you up for certain failure. The Final Draft website goes even further, calling for an "insanely detailed" outline that "even describes what the dialogue will be in every scene."[1]

MYTH #3 DEBUNKED!
Outlines Are Overrated and Can Stifle the Free Flow of Your Creativity

Remember Myth #1? There can be no absolutes where creativity is concerned, and dogma of any kind forces your words and story into a straitjacket of preconceptions and expectations.

DITCH THAT OUTLINE!

When I confess during screenwriting workshops I'm facilitating that I never outline, there are two opposing reactions from the group: a disapproving gasp from more conservative screenwriters and relieved sighs from the outline-challenged.

I have always fallen into the latter category. Back in school when required to hand in an outline with my essays and term papers, I always

---

[1] "How to Outline Your Screenplay," Final Draft website (http://www.finaldraft.com/learn/articles/how-to-outline-your-screenplay).

wrote the paper first. Unconscious rebel that I was, only then did I craft an outline to match it. Not much has changed in the years since: I have outlined none of my books and none of my screenplays.

For me, the outline is an intellectual exercise that constrains my creative flow and hurls mud into the crystal waters of my Muse Stream. Worse, it places me in the driver's seat of a journey that I know myself to be ill-equipped to navigate on my own.

An outline's gift and curse is that it provides you with a roadmap, which in turn sets out a destination for you to journey toward. Certainly, it's comforting and potentially more efficient to know where you're headed. An outline, however, also carries risks: It can remove serendipity and surprise from the experience if you hew to it unwaveringly, if you cling to it controllingly.

A few years ago on Facebook, a fellow writer challenged my attitude toward outlines. His argument went something like this: "The problem a lot of writers have is not being able to nail down exactly what their ending is before they start. That would be like getting in the car for a weekend getaway and not having any idea where you're going...just driving aimlessly, wasting a whole hell of a lot of gas. That's the value of a map, of an outline: If you know where you're going, you will get there, and usually in the most direct line."

It's ironic that my colleague used the "unmapped drive" analogy to criticize what he sees as the wastefulness of unplotted writing. Taking a random, unplanned drive is the example I often use in my classes and coaching sessions to celebrate the magic of exploration and discovery.

In my universe, it's more fun to get in the car, start it up and see where it will take me. Nearly always, it takes me to a place I never could have imagined going, along a route I never would have thought of traveling. That unmapped drive is a near-perfect metaphor for both how I write and how I live my life. Can it be scary sometimes? Certainly. Can it feel out-of-control? Absolutely. But those are the places where enchantment dwells, where astonishment resides, where miracles thrive. And what is life and creativity if not an enchanted journey of wonder, miracle and surprise?

When I write, I sit in the passenger seat of the experience; I leave the steering wheel to the story. I do that because I view the story as its own sentient entity, one that knows its direction and raison d'être far better than I ever could. I know that if I let it take charge, it will introduce me to ideas, characters, situations and scenes that my conscious mind would never have thought up...or permitted.

My only job is to get out of the way and trust the driver. My only job is to surrender to the journey.

If the Muse Stream is about trust and surrender, it's also about intuition. It's about recognizing that at a deep level you already know the story you have been called on to write and you already know the best way to put it into screenplay form. The Muse Stream is about listening to the innate wisdom and inner vision that resides deep within each of us. It's about trusting that wisdom and vision, unconditionally.

When we allow ourselves to surrender to that intuitive process, we don't need outlines. We need only one word, then the next, then the next, in the moment-to-moment unveiling that is the gift of the Muse Stream.

That doesn't make outlining wrong. There are no absolutes in creativity — no absolute rights and no absolute wrongs. Your responsibility as screenwriter-creator is to be open to whichever tools, techniques, processes, rhythms and routines reveal themselves to you and to adopt the ones the work best for you. It's also your responsibility to not get stuck in any of them. Recognize, as I noted in "Rhythms and Routines," that what works for you today on one draft or screenplay might not be appropriate tomorrow on another.

The key in this as in all things is to serve the screenplay not our perceived need to control it, which is too often what an outline ends up being about.

If you feel you must outline, don't treat the result as gospel. View it instead as a general trajectory from which you are free to stray — randomly, wildly, illogically and frequently. Consider, too, outlining on the Muse Stream, which is more an exercise in brainstorming than in point-by-point outlining. How? Go nonlinear with techniques such as free association or mind mapping and let the exercise be one of expansion, rather than constriction, of revelation rather than rote. Or plant a Word Tree, using the exercise that follows.

THE WORD TREE

A Word Tree[2] is a nonlinear type of outline, designed to open your mind to fresh ideas and new possibilities. Here's how to plant your own.

In the center of a large piece of blank, unlined paper, print your

---

[2] The Word Tree is based on the clustering technique developed and popularized by Gabriele Lusser Rico in her landmark book, *Writing the Natural Way* (Tarcher/Penguin, 1983, 2002).

screenplay's title (or if you don't yet have one, write "My Screenplay") and draw a circle around it. This is the trunk of your Word Tree.

Now, without stopping to think, analyze, criticize or judge, write the first word or phrase that leaps to mind, whether or not it's logically connected to your title. Circle your new word, link it with a line to the title and continue — by quickly writing, circling and linking the words triggered by each new association. See each circled word or phrase as a leaf and each connecting line as a branch on this Word Tree you are cultivating and growing. Continue free-associating in this way until you feel complete with a particular branch. Then, either return to your title or begin a new branch from any word or phrase you have already jotted down. Keep going for 5, 10 or 15 minutes, or until you have a sense that your Word Tree has grown to maturity.

Once your Word Tree is complete, scan the page — again, not with your critical or analytical mind. Do it instead from a right-brained, intuitive place. As you do, be open to any thoughts or ideas about your story and screenplay that your Word Tree might trigger. Note them if appropriate.

Now scan the page again. This time let a word or phrase bubble up from your unconscious. It could be a word or phrase that jumps out at you from the Word Tree or it could be something else altogether. Whatever it is, jot it down and let it be the kickoff to an experience in writing on the Muse Stream.

Write nonstop for 15 to 20 minutes, setting a timer should that be helpful. Let what emerges be whatever it is — a full scene, snatches of action or dialogue, a piece of narrative prose or a piece of writing about your story or screenplay. Remember to write nonstop, without pausing to correct spelling, punctuation or grammar, to hunt for the "right" word or to fuss about proper screenplay format. Remember, too, that if you feel stuck, you can use the "Write Anything" tips in "Navigating the Muse Stream When You Feel Stuck" (Scene 2) to reinitiate the flow.

When your time is up, set your writing aside for at least an hour. Take a walk or do something else unrelated to your script. Then, when you feel able to look at what you have written uncritically and without judgment, read it — with an open heart and mind — and see what it adds to your screenplay or what it tells you about your screenplay, about yourself or about both. While this exercise is not specifically designed to produce direct content for your script, it may.

Return to this exercise any time you feel the need for a kick-start, fresh ideas or any kind of inspirational boost.

Myth #4: "If I Don't Control My Story and its Characters, I Will Never Write a Coherent Script"

Some writers fear that unless they retain an uncompromising grip on their story, they are guaranteed a plot that's disjointed, characters who are inconsistent and a screenplay that is thematically uneven and structurally unsound.

Not so. The more you trust your story and its characters, the richer and more engaging will be your final script.

MYTH #4 DEBUNKED!
Control Is a Creativity-Stifling Illusion

More often than we are comfortable admitting, our creativity can't begin to express its full potential until the moment we stop trying to control it and instead let the story we are writing take charge.

Novelist E.L. Doctorow writes, "Writing is like driving at night in the fog. You can only see as far as your headlights, but you can make the whole trip that way."

As we move forward, writing the word, sentence or scene we know, the next will always appear...if we are open to it. If we have our eyes on the road and have our headlights switched on, if we are prepared to trust in the unknown that lies just beyond the reach of our vision, that unknown will become illuminated, known and manifest.

There's a scene in *The MoonQuest* book and screenplay that reminds me of Doctorow's quote. In it, the main character is walking a celestial road that only forms with each step he takes. The road behind him has vanished and the road beyond each next step cannot be discerned. As stressful and discomfiting as he finds the journey, the road takes him where he needs to go: to a place he could never have imagined.

That's the same journey I traveled in writing *The MoonQuest*, a story I knew nothing about except as I wrote it. Some days Doctorow's headlights revealed the next scene. Some days, only the next sentence. Some days, only the next word. Yet as I surrendered to the journey — and to the voice of my Muse — the story unfolded, magnificently, and in ways I could not have predicted, plotted or envisioned.

A few years ago an artist came to me with the painter's equivalent of writer's block. She sensed a new style birthing through her but didn't know how to access it. All she could do was stare at her blank canvas in mounting frustration.

"Your only job is to hold the brush," I told her during one of our coaching sessions, "because that's the one thing your painting can't do on its own. If you get out of the way and trust the brush to move your hand across the canvas, your painting will reveal itself to you."

She did, and it did. It's no different with your screenplay.

In the end, as I noted when debunking Myth #3, the Muse Stream is about trust. It's about trusting that if you move from the driver's seat of your story experience to its passenger seat, you will free onto the page a screenplay that is more imaginative than anything you could have thought up.

Creativity — and screenwriting *is* a creative process — is not a logical enterprise you can control. Creativity is about weird leaps of faith that often make no sense in the moment. In fact, what seems to be nonsense in the moment may turn out to be the most brilliant aspect of your screenplay by the time you type FADE OUT on the final page.

So get out of the way and let your story have its way with you. Let the words of action and dialogue spill out of you — the words your screenplay needs, not the words you think it needs. Not the words you think you need. Abandon control and free your story to live its full potential, a potential your conscious imagination can only begin to touch.

Myth #5: "I Can't Start Writing If I Don't Know How My Screenplay Begins... and Ends"

How many times have you heard that you must know what your story is about (or, at the very least, have a sense of your protagonist's character arc) before you start writing?

How many times have you heard that you must know your screenplay's final scene before you can write its first one?

How many times have you heard that unless you "write to the ending," your screenplay will be disjointed, its trajectory muddy and its climax unsatisfying?

Of course, there's nothing wrong with starting out with a clear sense of your story, its main character and its ending. But you don't need *any* of them in order to get started.

MYTH #5 DEBUNKED!
Your Story Will Guide You, If You Let It

That's what the Muse Stream is all about. You don't have a storyline, theme, characters or opening scene? Pick a word, any word, and just start. Keep writing without stopping, and *don't think*. You don't know how your screenplay is going to end? You don't have to. Perhaps it's even better if you don't.

All you need to know in this moment is the next word. Just one word. Any word. It doesn't matter what that word is. If you write on the Muse Stream, if you trust, if you put your faith in the superior wisdom of your story and surrender to that story, that one word will take you where you need to go. Always.

Your sole responsibility is to begin.

So begin.

Your sole responsibility is to continue.

So continue.

Drop a word onto the page. Then another. And another. Follow the words where they take you. Let them open up into conversations and conflicts, into scenes and acts, as they reveal your story to you...the story only you can write.

Myth #6: "I Must Know Everything About My Characters Before Starting"

This is a myth that transcends media and genres, one that novelists and playwrights hear as often as do screenwriters. It's false across the board.

MYTH #6 DEBUNKED!
Your Characters Will Reveal Themselves to You as You Write, If You Let Them

Just as you can trust your story to reveal itself to you, you can trust your characters to do the same. If you free your story's men, women and children to live out their own imperative in their own way, you will endow them with a humanity and an authenticity that will be more engaging to your audience (not to mention to prospective actors and producers) than if you preplan and plot out every aspect of their lives.

See "Screenplay Craft: Getting Into Character" (Scene 6) for more about character development.

Myth #7: "I Must Write My Screenplay in Story Order"

Even if you believe yourself to be writing your script in story order, that order could shift in the next draft...and again in the one after that. Then, of course, depending on what happens in postproduction during editing, the final film's scene order may not resemble anything in any of your drafts. So don't worry! In this as in all aspects of your screenwriting enterprise, let the story come as it comes...and write it that way.

MYTH #7 DEBUNKED!
Your Story Will Find Its Own Sequence, If You Let It

Sometimes, writing a scene out of sequence — intentionally or not — can reveal to you aspects of your story or its characters that you might otherwise have overlooked or have taken longer to discover. This happened to me while working on *The StarQuest* and *The SunQuest*, when I crafted scenes that not only ended up being out-of-sequence but out-of-script: Scenes intended for one screenplay found their way into the other and vice-versa.

Sometimes, too, if you recall from "Navigating the Muse Stream When You Feel Stuck" (Scene 2), postponing a challenging scene can help keep you writing when you hit a roadblock.

Myth #8: "Master Dialogue and I Will Master Screenwriting"

Years ago when I was studying for my business degree, I remember a marketing professor telling the class that the best way to assess a TV commercial was to switch off the sound. "If you still get the message and feel the emotion of it with no sound," he said, "you know you've got an effective and persuasive commercial."

It's similar in film. The days of silent movies may be long gone, but we still tend to respond more viscerally to what we see than to what we hear.

MYTH #8 DEBUNKED!
There's More to Accomplished Screenwriting than Dialogue

Dialogue that reveals character, evokes emotion and tells story is critical to every film. But so is everything else you see on the screen.

As a screenwriter you are more than a speechwriter; you are a visual artist, a painter. Your job is to transform your screenplay pages into canvases upon which you paint the word pictures that conjure up a motion picture. It takes more than dialogue to do that.

More about the importance of expressive action paragraphs when I debunk Myth #9 ("My Screenplay Is Only a Blueprint for the Final Film: Evocative Writing Doesn't Matter").

See also "Screenplay Craft: Getting Into Character" (Scene 6) for more about dialogue.

TRY THIS
Follow my marketing prof's advice and mute the soundtrack from any

film that is not a talking-heads feature (e.g., *My Dinner with Andre*). Note how much you are able to discern and feel from what you see — from the settings, cinematography and lighting and from the actors' actions and expressions.

As a variation on this exercise, keep the soundtrack playing but pay attention to all the sequences that have few lines or none. Are there more of those than you expected? Where there is little or no dialogue, again note all the other elements of the scene — setting, music, action and nonverbal cues. What to do they reveal to you about the story and its characters? What emotions are these scenes able to evoke in you? Would dialogue have heightened or weakened your emotional response?

TRY THIS TOO

Using one of the prompts from "Sixty Story-Starters" (Scene 5), write a short scene. When you have finished, rewrite the scene, eliminating all or most of the dialogue.

TRY THIS AS WELL

If you have an existing script or a screenplay-in-progress, find a dialogue-heavy scene and rewrite it. As in the previous exercise, find ways to eliminate all or most of the dialogue without diluting the scene's power and impact.

Myth #9: "My Screenplay Is Only a Blueprint for the Final Film: Evocative Writing Doesn't Matter"

A blueprint is a precisely detailed document that converts an architect's vision into a strict plan for builders and contractors. While a screenplay also sets out a vision for the writer's story, it is more than a mechanical how-to for director, actors and designers. Perhaps a more apt metaphor would be an artist's rendering, with its shapes and shadings, its eloquence and flair.

Just because the screenplay form demands brief sentences and paragraphs doesn't mean that your script is not a literary work...is not a literary work designed to be *read*. Before it is ever viewed on a cinema screen, your script's first audience is always going to be an audience of readers.

MYTH #9 DEBUNKED!
Evocative Writing Matters

Your job, as I pointed out when debunking Myth #8, is to paint the word pictures that will seduce everyone who reads your screenplay — from the freelance reader scaling a sky-scraping tower of unsolicited scripts to the producer, actors, director and production designer who will ultimately realize it on the screen.

As such, good writing matters. Powerful writing matters. Evocative writing matters.

Never hesitate to seek out more forceful and expressive ways to translate your vision onto the page. One way is to replace adjectives with robust nouns and adverbs with dynamic verbs. For those adjectives and adverbs that remain necessary, choose modifiers that more effectively express your intent.

If evocative writing matters, so does concise writing — more in screenwriting than in any other literary genre. Unlike a novelist, a screenwriter doesn't have the space to allow a single description to spill lyrically into multiple paragraphs. Even a short-story writer has more freedom in this regard than you do. Be powerful but spare in your use of language.

Compact writing that packs a punch isn't easy: "I have made this letter longer," Blaise Pascal wrote five centuries ago, "because I have not had the time to make it shorter." In early drafts, give yourself permission to let your descriptions and dialogue run long. Use later drafts to trim the fat.

TRY THIS

Take the following 55-word description from *The MoonQuest* script and tighten it as much as you can, without stripping it of interest and important information.

```
Toshar wakes up. He is reclining against the trunk
of a broad, ancient tree, which sits at the center
of a plateau that is, itself, suspended far above
the suns and clouds. The plateau is shaped like an
irregular circle and is studded with colorful wild-
flowers. He sees no way back down to the ground.³
```

Compare your version with the 27-word original in the footnote.

TRY THIS TOO

If you don't already have one, get a Twitter account and practice writing posts of substance that don't exceed the social network's 280-characters-or-less requirement. If you're more ambitious, try limiting your tweets to the network's previous limit of 140 characters or less.

Look for more evocative-writing tips in "The Edit Suite" (Scene 11).

---

³ Original description: "Toshar wakes under a broad, ancient tree in the center of an irregularly circular, flower-studded plateau far above suns and clouds. He sees no way down."

Myth #10: "Three-Act Structure Matters: I Have to Map Out My Acts"

Most screenwriting books and courses go on at length about "three-act structure" and about how your script must conform to that formula. In those same books and classes, you will also hear a lot about "beats" and "plot points" and about how you must work these out with technical precision *before* you start writing.

"Must," as I suggested when debunking Myth #1, has no place in a creative artist's vocabulary or work habits.

MYTH #10 DEBUNKED!
All That Matters Is Your Story

Your screenplay and its structure exist to serve your story and its ultimate translation into film, not the other way around. Story is king, not structure.

When you write on the Muse Stream and are in tune with your characters, story and script, your three acts will emerge on their own, naturally and intuitively, as will many of your beats and plot points. There is no need to plan, plot, engineer or graph them. And while they will likely need to be tweaked in future drafts, the revision process can be just as intuitive, if you get out of the way of your screenplay's innate wisdom.

See "The Edit Suite" (Scene 11) for more about revision.

THE MYTH OF ACTS AND BEATS

For director Fred Zinnemann, a film resembles the flow of a symphony, rather than the artificiality and choppiness of acts: "I am never one for feeling that a film should be subdivided into acts," he told George Stevens Jr. in *Conversations with the Great Moviemakers of Hollywood's Golden Age at the American Film Institute*. "That's something we've dragged in from the theater."

And a note about the origin of "beats," as it relates to actors and scripts: In her book *Directing Actors*[4], Judith Weston suggests that the term goes back to the 1920s, when the great Russian director Constantin Stanislavsky was asked how he worked on scenes with actors. "Beet by beet," he is said to have replied in heavily accented English, meaning "bit by bit." Before long, Weston writes, Stanislavsky's response morphed into actor-speak's "working with beats."

Whether true or not — Weston describes the story as apocryphal — it demonstrates how easily a random remark can congeal into gospel.

Once again: Story is king, not structure.

---

[4] While targeted at directors, Weston's books include many insights that are equally relevant for screenwriters.

Myth #11: "Screenplay Format Matters: I Have to Master Proper Format Before I Can Start Writing"

When it comes to screenplays, each element — from slug lines to action and from character names to dialogue — must look a certain way, and the whole thing must be typed in a Courier font. Certain words or phrases must be capitalized, abbreviated or placed in parentheses. Some parts of your screenplay must be precisely indented, some must be indented even more; some must be written at the left margin and some must be written at the right margin.

The catalogue of screenplay-format dos and don'ts can feel overwhelming and can, if you let it, get it in the way of your creative output.

Don't let it get in the way.

MYTH #11 DEBUNKED!
Format Matters in Your Screen*play*, not in Your Screen*writing*

What do I mean by that? You will want to make certain that the final draft of your screen*play* adheres to the requisite industry dictates. You don't need to worry about those dictates while you are screen*writing*.

Manage your script's format as best you can while writing and in your early revisions. Later, devote a draft specifically to tidying up your format to meet industry standards.

While screenwriting software isn't mandatory (I composed the first draft of *The MoonQuest* script using Apple's Pages program and a screenplay template I found online), a professional screenwriting program like Final Draft or Movie Magic will remove much of the guesswork and stress from the formatting enterprise.

Screenwriting software, however, won't answer all your questions, so you will still want to pick up a reputable book on format to help guide you.

Yet even with something as seemingly doctrinaire as film-script format, you will find variations from one book to another. Here, as everywhere else in life and creativity, you will never achieve perfection. It's just not possible!

See Screenwriting Rule #8 for more about perfection.

Myth #12: "Market Trends Matter: I Have to Write What's Selling Now"

Go to the movies or tune in to your favorite streaming service and pay attention to current releases. Read *Variety* and other trade publications if you want to keep up with industry news and trends. But don't let what you see and what you read affect your choice of topic, theme and story. Don't let it get in the way of what you are going to write today.

MYTH #12 DEBUNKED!

The Market Is Fickle: Today's Trends Are Irrelevant

The stories that producers seek today are unlikely to be the same ones they will be optioning by the time you have finished your screenplay. The market is volatile. Producers are capricious. Today's trends will not resemble tomorrow's.

Or as Oscar-winning screenwriter William Goldman noted about the film industry, "Nobody knows anything."

On the other hand, what your heart calls to you to write in this moment may be just what captures a producer's attention in two months, six months or a year. The story your Muse sends you today may be just the story that makes the public pulse race when your film is released a year or two after that.

Write what you must write right now, and trust your story and your Muse to find its right home in its right time.

Myth #13: "I'm Not Good Enough or Creative Enough to Write This Story"

This is the biggest and most pernicious myth of all, and it affects all creative artists at one time or another.

MYTH #13 DEBUNKED!
You Are Good Enough and Creative Enough to Write *Your* Story

You are good enough because everyone is good enough. Everyone carries the seeds of creation within them. As director Ron Howard put it, "We're all creative."

Besides, if a story has chosen you to write it, then it is *your* story to write, which means that you must be good enough to do it. Can you trust that?

You have judged yourself as wanting long enough. Let your judgment go and watch the Muse Stream flow!

LET JUDGMENT GO: A GUIDED MEDITATION

Allow at least 30 minutes for this meditation and for the writing experience that flows from it.

A professionally recorded meditation similar to this one is available for download or streaming[5]. See "Getting Started" (Scene 1) for details on how to access the recording, as well as for tips on how best to use this book's meditations.

Breathe. Breathe in the quiet, white light of your creative essence, your

---

[5] Search the relevant site/store for "Mark David Gerson let judgment go"

divine essence, your Muse. Breathe in your fire, your flame, your being-ness, your God-self. Breathe in the light of who you are, the truth of who you are, the love of who you are. Breathe in all the light and aloha you are.

Aloha is not just a word that conjures up the gentle swaying of palm trees and hula dancers. Aloha is a consciousness, a state of being, a state of open-heartedness, a state of love in its truest, fullest sense.

Breathe in to that openness within you. Breathe it in fully, deeply, completely.

Breathe out any doubts, any fears that you're not good enough, that someone else or anyone else is a more accomplished creator. Breathe that out, for it is not true.

You are creative. You are innately creative. You are inherently creative. Everyone is. And because you are, you can express that creativity through writing, through screenwriting, through placing one word after the next and one scene after the next on the written page.

Let go of all feelings that you're not good enough. For you are. Release all feelings that others are better than you. They are not. You are equal to all and equal to the joyful task at hand, which is expressing the words and passions of your heart in written form. You are equal to it, for you were born to it. Every micro-bit, every nano-bit of your being — physical, emotional and spiritual — has been encoded with that will, desire and aptitude to create.

You may lack certain skills. Those skills can be learned and prac-ticed. In this moment, skills don't matter nearly as much as heart, intent and choice. You have the former. We all do. And you can tap into the latter two with ease.

Know that and be that.

It's simple. It's simple yet complex, for you are pushing against what may seem like lifetimes of programming.

What has been programmed can be erased — more quickly than the time it took to program into you.

You are good enough. You are better than good enough.

Despite what anyone ever said, despite any way in which you were treated — words and actions your conscious mind may have long ago forgotten or buried — despite any or all of these, you are a writer, a screenwriter.

You *are* good enough. Your words are good enough. Your scripted creations are good enough. Better than good enough. For they are the unique expressions of a unique heart that is, even now, opening to the prospect and possibility of finally being free to speak.

Feel that freedom. Open to that freedom. Embrace that freedom. It needn't frighten you. It needn't close you down. It is safe. For in that freedom lies all the truth of the universe, just as within you lies all the truth of the universe.

So put pen to paper, let fingers dance upon the keyboard and simply begin. Begin at the beginning. Let that first word be the God of the Old Testament, who allowed the world to form. "Let there be light," God said. Not, "I order and command light." Not, "The light must look a certain way, must be a certain brightness."

Creation is an act of allowing, of letting. *Let* there be light. *Let* there be creation. *Let* there be one story, and then another. And let the words that best express that story find their own way onto the page, without any need by you to intervene or get in the way.

Let. Let the words be. Let yourself be. There is no judging in the act of letting. There is no call to judge. There is no call to take any active role whatsoever. Surrender to creation and let it be.

God didn't say as the earth formed, "You know, I don't like this island over here and that mountain over there." God allowed the earth to form and saw it, and it was good. God didn't judge it to be good. By allowing, it was good. Inherently good. Allow your creations to form without judgment, and they too will be good.

Give your creations life. Then give them the free will to form as they will, to live their imperative.

Let. Let them form. Let them be. Let them love you. Let yourself love them back.

There is no need to judge. There is never any need to judge. Let the words flow and let judgment go. Let it fly…far, far away where it can do no more damage or harm to you or your words or your work. Or to anyone or anything.

Now, pick a word, any word. Let a word or phrase bubble up into your consciousness. A word that expresses your state of beingness in this moment.

Don't judge it. Never judge. Don't censor it. Never censor. Allow. Simply allow.

And when that word or phrase has emerged, let that be your starting point, your launching pad, your rocket, propelling you to the farthest reaches of the universe in a free-flowing flight of creation.

And so, write. Right now. Write in free-flowing prose or in screen-play format. For the purposes of this exercise, it doesn't matter. Write whatever and however the words come.

Remember to keep your pen moving across the page or your fingers flying along the keyboard. Let the words race onto your page or screen. Free those words and the words will free you.

Let them fly and let yourself fly with them.

If you feel stuck, just keep going. Repeat. Free-associate. Write nonsense. Breathe. Any or all of these will release the stuckness and propel you forward.

Write for as long as you can, until you feel complete, and then for a little bit longer if that feels right.

Write. Now.

Scene 4.
12½ "Rules" for Writing Your Screenplay

FRANK CAPRA (THREE-TIME OSCAR WINNER FOR BEST DIRECTOR)

The whole thing is you've got to make them care about somebody.

INGMAR BERGMAN (WRITER/DIRECTOR & NINE-TIME OSCAR NOMINEE)

Very often the personalities in my scripts don't want the same thing I want. If I try to force them to do what I want to do, it will always be an artistic catastrophe.

I wrote the original version of these rules more than a decade ago for my first book for writers, "The Voice of the Muse: Answering the Call to Write." Since then, I have adapted them multiple times for different creative media, genres and forms. Yet through its myriad variants, two things about my list of so-called rules never change: My first and last will always remind you that the only right way is the one that works for you today and that nothing innovative or groundbreaking was ever conjured up by consenting to be bound by someone else's rules, mandates or ways of doing things.

The "Rules"

1. There are no rules

2. Your story knows best

3. Your story is a trickster

4. If the Muse Stream is good enough for Francis Ford Coppola, it should be good enough for you

5. Go for the jugular

6. Write your passion

7. Write what you know…if you dare

8. Strive for excellence, not perfection

9. Write!

10. Respect every word and draft

11. Set yourself up for success

12. Empower yourself

12½. Rules? Oh, yeah. There are none.

Rule #1: There Are No Rules

Many people will tell you that screenwriting is all about rules. They're wrong.

If you write anything based on rulebooks and the way things "should be," "must be" or "are supposed to be," you will produce work that is at best formulaic, manipulative and derivative. And you will be writing to today's tastes, trends and views, not to the ones that will be in effect when your screenplay is finished and produced.

Of course, there are industry requirements you must adhere to if you are going to submit your spec screenplay for consideration. Mostly, these relate to page count, font and format. While these requirements may seem rigid or even archaic, they are no more strict than the guidelines set down by publishers for book manuscripts or by galleries for artist submissions.

The "rules" of submission stipulated by agents, producers and competition judges, however, have nothing to do with your story, which brings us to Rule #2. But before we get there…

ASK YOURSELF THESE QUESTIONS

- What "rules" about writing and screenwriting do I follow?

- Whose rules are they?

- How have those rules served my screenwriting enterprise? How have they held me back, stifled my creativity or even sabotaged me?

- Which of those rules can I break, today?

Commit to start breaking some of those rules, today!

Rule #2: Your Story Knows Best

I knew nothing about *The SunQuest* story when I typed FADE IN at the top of its first screenplay page some years back. Well, that's not entirely true: I was pretty sure I knew who the main character was going to be and that the story would somehow continue the saga that I had initiated with *The MoonQuest* and *The StarQuest*. That was it. I didn't know how *The SunQuest* would begin. I didn't know how it would end. And I didn't know what would fill that vast Act II void in between.

(Although those three *Q'ntana* stories are linked, each has a largely independent plot and cast of characters. And although *The MoonQuest* and *StarQuest* scripts were adapted from far-from-final drafts of the novels, I wrote *The SunQuest* first as a screenplay, then novelized it.)

As you already know from my debunking of Myth #3 in the previous section, I never outline my stories. As well, I rarely plan or make notes before starting a writing project. So what did I do?

I listened *for* the story. I listened *to* the story. I trusted what I heard, and I began to write.

After FADE IN, I typed EXT. (I had a fifty percent chance of being right!) and continued the slug line with a single word: CASTLE. "Castle" led to another word, then to another after that…and to another and another…until I had a scene. That scene, too, led to another and then to another…and then to another one after that.

With each word I learned more about the story. With each scene I learned more about its characters. And as the scenes collected themselves into acts and ultimately into a completed draft, I began to see how *The SunQuest* fit within the larger opus that was *The Legend of Q'ntana* and how clues I had unconsciously planted in its *MoonQuest* and *StarQuest* predecessors were now playing out, as if consciously plotted and planned, in the series' third installment.

If I have learned anything over my decades of writing, it's that my stories are smarter than I am. Infinitely smarter.

The first time I became aware of this was when I was struggling through that first draft of *The MoonQuest*; struggling because I was reluctant to surrender fully to the Muse Stream. I remember how the story would often want to veer off in a direction that seemed to make no sense. My first inclination was to resist this plot turn. Yet if I didn't, if I followed the story where it wanted to go rather than forcing it to my will, it *always* worked out. Not only did it work out, it did so in ways that were far more engaging, dramatic and thematically relevant than anything I could have tried to figure out, plan or make up.

Your story knows itself better than you ever will. Your story knows its ideal form, shape and structure. Your story knows its characters, situations, conflicts and settings. Your story knows its theme. I would even venture to say that your story knows its ultimate destination and fate.

Your job is to get out of the story's way — and your own — and let it have its way with you. Your job is to let your screenplay write itself.

If you let it, it will.

SURRENDER TO THE JOURNEY

Let your screenplay be a voyage of discovery...for you as much as for your ultimate viewer.

In June 1997, I embarked on an odyssey whose consequences I could never have predicted...or imagined. I had been back living in Toronto for only a short while when, during an early morning walk, an inner voice urged me to pack the little I owned into the back of my Dodge Caravan and head west.

At other times in my life, I would have questioned my sanity. That morning, I knew that my only choice was to listen, trust and surrender.

I left the city a few weeks later, never knowing where I would drive next, never knowing where I would end up...or when.

From Toronto I traveled north and west along the rugged, forested shores of Lake Huron and Lake Superior, then south and west, crossing Minnesota, North Dakota, South Dakota, Wyoming, Montana, Idaho and Oregon. From the Oregon coast, I slipped south into California, then shot back east, across Nevada and Utah, before dropping into northern Arizona.

It was a magically transformative experience, though not without stress, for it was difficult at times to surrender fully. Part of me longed to plot out an itinerary, to know where I would drive the next week, to know how this open-ended pilgrimage would end. The greater, more courageous part of me trusted in the infinite wisdom of the journey.

Through all the unexpected stops, unanticipated detours and unpredicted forays into uncharted territory, all I could do was trust in each moment and trust as well that the story I was living would reveal itself... through the living of it.

It did, magnificently.

After ninety days of traveling, I drove into Sedona, Arizona, expecting this to be another whistle stop on the road to wherever. Instead, one week grew to two, one month to seven. Before I knew it, I had a new country and a new wife, and a new baby was on the way.

Had I given my brain-mind the control it sought, I might never have left Toronto, might never have launched an adventure that gifted me so richly...that continues to gift me.

Part of what prepared me for that odyssey was *The MoonQuest*, a novel whose early drafts I had written much as I lived those three months: moment-by-moment and word-by-word, ignorant of the outcome but trusting that one would emerge that was worthy of the experience. More than a dozen years later, that's how I would write the first draft of my *SunQuest* screenplay.

When we surrender to our heart-mind, trusting that the outcome will be more wondrous than anything we could consciously imagine, it always is. When we surrender to our Muse and to our story, the same is true.

TRY THIS

As you write today, notice all the times your mind edges (or leaps) ahead of the word or scene you are writing to try to figure out what's coming next or how the story will end. Notice it, but don't punish yourself for it. Simply return your focus to the word of the moment and continue writing, in the moment. Let your story carry you as my car did me — in trust and surrender. Let it carry you to the story you didn't know you knew, as breath by breath you move toward an outcome that has yet to reveal itself.

TRY THIS TOO

Have you ever started your car and simply taken off, with no clear itinerary and no fixed destination? Have you ever gone for an aimless walk, just to see where your feet would carry you? Have you ever boarded a bus, subway or commuter train with no plan other than to enjoy the ride, wherever it takes you? Now is the time to try any or all of those unplanned, unplotted experiences.

Without attempting anything as dramatic as the three-month open-ended road odyssey I described above, switch off your cellphone and, if you're driving, your vehicle's GPS, and take off. Walk, drive, bicycle, take public transit or mix 'n match your modes of transportation. Give yourself a full morning or afternoon or, if you can spare it, a full day. Stop somewhere you've never been for coffee or a meal. Strike up a conversation with a stranger. Pop into a store or a park or a museum or some other site of conventional or unconventional interest along the way, preferably a place you're visiting for the first time. And do your best to not return along the same route.

When you get back, answer these questions...

- Where did you go? What did you see? What did you discover?

- What did you discover about yourself?

- What was fun about it?

- What was less fun or even stressful about it?

- Who did you talk to and what did you talk about?

- What it would feel like if you gave yourself permission to plan less and surrender more in your everyday life? In your writing life?

Rule #3: Your Story Is a Trickster

The Trickster is a mythological and archetypal figure that dupes its victims into doing its bidding. Mischievous by nature, it will lie unashamedly and break any rule to get its own way.

In myth, think leprechauns (Ireland), coyotes (US Southwest), the Greek god Dionysus, the Hawaiian/Polynesian demigod Maui and the Norse god Loki.

In literature and legend, think Puss in Boots, Br'er Rabbit, *A Midsummer Night's Dream*'s Puck and every court jester ever conceived, including *King Lear*'s Fool.

In more recent times, Bugs Bunny, Wile E. Coyote, the Pink Panther, Q in *Star Trek: The Next Generation* and even Bart Simpson could be considered tricksters.

Your story and your Muse are also tricksters. As you craft the screenplay you think you are writing, they will often trick you into writing something you never expected to write, something you never thought you wanted to write, something you never thought you could write.

This is good.

Curse, mutter and resist if you must. Then surrender to your story's higher wisdom. It *is* smarter than you are and it will always take you not only to the place of creative magic, awe and wonder but to the place where your screenplay's ideal expression resides.

Rule #4: If the Muse Stream Is Good Enough for Francis Ford Coppola, It Should Be Good Enough for You

The Muse Stream, as I pointed out a few sections back, is about writing without stopping. Not stopping to correct spelling, punctuation or grammar. Not stopping to edit. Not stopping to grope for the right word or correct format. Not stopping to worry whether a piece of dialogue is right or whether a piece of action is too long or too short. The Muse Stream is about always moving forward — to the next word, to the next piece of dialogue, to the next scene.

What does that have to do with Francis Ford Coppola? As the Oscar-winning screenwriter of *The Godfather* works on a screenplay, he never looks back over what he has already written and he never rewrites until he is ready to start his next draft. He just keeps moving forward. George Lucas is said to work the same way.

"You have a lot of doubts when you read in unfinished fragments," Coppola told *Creative Screenwriting* magazine in 2009. "There's almost a hormone that secretes from writers to hate what they're writing, so you get fooled into reworking and changing it."

Surrendering to the Muse Stream means going with first thoughts, committing to the page whatever leaps first into your mind, however wacky it might seem. In fact, the wackier it seems, the more likely it is that your inner censor is interfering with your creative process.

"Wacky" is a judgment. It comes from that fearful, second-thoughts, second-guessing part of you that is trying to protect you from straying into dangerous territory, that is afraid you will be judged harshly for what you are about to write.

The Muse Stream — writing without stopping — is designed to bypass that inner critic and get your most creative thoughts onto the page before those logical, analytical, critical, cynical, doubt-filled or judgmental parts of you can stop them.

"It's counterproductive," notes Coppola, "to start judging it before you've allowed the whole trip to take place."

That's the creative reason for surrendering to the Muse Stream. But there is also a practical reason.

What if you start your screenplay and before moving forward to Scene 2, you spend days and weeks polishing, perfecting and otherwise tweaking your first-draft opening scene (a scene that you're convinced is so brilliant that it will earn you, the actors, the director and the film a constellation of Oscars)?

There's nothing wrong with that, right? Who doesn't want an Oscar?

But what if, when you begin your second draft, you realize that your opening scene is not as brilliant as you had originally thought? What if, as you reread those weeks of work, you realize that, not only is it not brilliant, it's not even salvageable? As you hold down the delete key over the entire scene, you will be thinking of all the time you could have put to better use had you surrendered to the Muse Stream, had you written without going back to rewrite, had you kept moving forward.

There is a time and place for revision and rewriting; it is not while you are in your Muse Stream's creative flow. And, as we shall see in "The Edit Suite" (Scene 11), revision need not be a slash-and-burn, left-brain assault on your screenplay. It can be as intuitive as your acts of creation — and just as effective.

BE IN THE MOMENT

As Francis Ford Coppola does, forget the words you have already written. Don't worry about the words yet to come. Focus only on the word you are writing. The next word will always come...if you don't worry about it. If you let it.

Be in the moment with each word...word by word. The word that trips off your fingers and onto the keyboard is the only one that matters. When you stop to think about each word, when you stop to analyze, judge and left-brain each word, you risk cutting off the next word.

It's just like with your breath. Do you worry about where your next breath is going to come from? Unless you suffer from some sort of respiratory disease, you never worry about your breath. You rarely think about your breath. You assume it will come and it does, moment-by-moment. One breath in one moment, then another in the next...then another in the one after that.

Your breath comes because you let it, because you don't get in its way, because you're not thinking about it or worrying about it.

The words of your screenplay can be like that too.

If you trust your story, the words always come. The words always come because they are already there. They're there because in some sense, your story already exists.

It exists in the same invisible realm in which your dreams, visions and ideas exist. And if you believe in that existence, if you trust in that existence, if you know deep in your heart that your story is already present and smarter than you are, and if you act from that knowingness, you will never lack the words your story needs for its expression.

So how do you get to that place where the story's words release from you as effortlessly as does your breath?

By writing. By writing without stopping...without stopping for any reason that could give your fault-finding self any opportunity for input during these initial, creative stages. By staying in the moment and surrendering to the Muse Stream.

Rule #5: Go for the Jugular

No, I'm not suggesting that you write like a pit bull primed for attack or that you adopt throat-slashing horror as your genre of choice. It's *your* jugular that I'm encouraging you to go for.

As you write, go for the feeling you would run from. Go for the emotion you would stuff. Go for the belief you would deny. Write about all the things you're scared of. Write about all the things you would give anything to avoid having to face. Get them on paper and strip them of their dominion over you. Get them on paper and free them to empower your characters, your screenplay and the movie.

Write, too, from the places that exhilarate and exasperate you. Write about your loves and your lusts, about your intoxications and your desperations, about your terrors and your taboos. Go as deep as you dare into your emotional life...then go deeper still...then deeper still. Once you have, put it all into the worlds and lives of your characters.

When we write from a place of powerful emotion, our writing can't help but act on our readers in powerful ways...in visceral ways.

"I'm not writing for readers," you say. Of course you are. As I noted when debunking Myth #9, the first audience for your screenplay is always going to be an audience of readers. From there, it will be up to actors, designers and a director to take the words they have experienced in your script and bring them to life on the screen. But if your words don't first leap off the page and grab those early readers by the throat, they will never make it onto the screen.

Rule #6: Write Your Passion

In the decade before *The MoonQuest* urged itself onto me, I was a Toronto freelance writer and editor, producing articles, brochures, reports, speeches and advertising copy that reflected someone else's thoughts and ideas, and I did it to meet someone else's deadlines. I was being paid to write, for which I was grateful. But I rarely wrote anything I cared deeply about, and had my Muse not whirled into my life when it did like a turbo-charged dervish, I don't know how much longer I could have continued without seizing up.

To borrow from mythologist Joseph Campbell, I had begun to follow my bliss, but my journey had stalled. I wasn't living my passion and I wasn't writing my passion. The lack of passion showed in my work, which, though technically proficient enough to keep the jobs coming in, was creatively stunted.

If screenwriting is just a job to you, as my freelance work was to me all those years ago, then Rule #6 may not apply to you. If that's your attitude toward writing, then this book probably doesn't apply to you either.

But if you are a screenwriter because you care about movies, because you care about stories and storytelling, and because you care about your audiences and want to have an impact on them — not to mention on your actors and director — then Rule #6 is a rule to heed.

Just to be clear: I am not urging you to preach, pontificate or manipulate. Film is an entertainment medium and your first job is to keep your audience interested and engaged.

Rather, I'm suggesting that you write what you're passionate about. As Karl Iglesias points out in *Writing for Emotional Impact*, "An idea should excite, energize, and electrify anyone who hears it." That's not going to happen unless it first excites, energizes and electrifies you. After all, why should anyone care deeply enough about your world and its characters to give you two hours of their life if you don't respect them enough to care just as deeply?

There is a world of "good ideas" out there. You will come across some online or in today's news headlines; your friends, neighbors and family will suggest others. But there's a difference between a "good" idea and the idea that is right for you right now.

Any writer can take a good idea and give it shape and substance. Some can do it better than you, some not as well. No one can take the idea that sings to your soul and perform the kind of alchemy on it that you can.

Be open to the idea that expresses your passion. Write the story you can't not write. Write it the way only you can.

ASK YOURSELF THESE QUESTIONS

How do I feel about the project I am working on right now? Am I as excited by it as I was when I started? If not, why not? What can I do to rekindle my passion? If I can't rekindle my passion, is this "write idea" the *right* idea for me right now? If it isn't, what could I be working on instead that would more fully energize and electrify me?

Rule #7: Write What You Know...If You Dare

Write what you know. How often have you heard that statement or one like it?

You can't write about a black man unless you're black.

You can't write about women if you're not a woman.

You can't write about pilots; you lack cockpit experience.

You can't write about a gay man or a lesbian because you're neither.

You can't write about the someone who's ninety because you're only twenty-two.

You can't write about someone from a different background, culture or country.

How often have statements like that frustrated you? Stifled you?

Consider this: How much research do you think Leonardo da Vinci did before he painted *The Last Supper?* The Bible tells the story, but it offers no physical description of that scene or those individuals.

Yet da Vinci knew *The Last Supper.* He knew it as well as if not better than any biblical source. He knew it in his heart. Not in his head, which would have cautioned him against attempting anything so audacious and out of his experience. But he had lived the emotions he represented and those emotions are the only truth that matters in that masterful painting.

So you have never experienced the discrimination a black woman or gay man might have felt? Have you ever been attacked for who you are? Have you ever been denied what you believed was rightfully yours? Have you ever felt your personhood and humanity under attack?

No? Think back to childhood, to the bullies in the schoolyard, to the adults who criticized you. Do more than think back. Relive and reexperience those moments. You *have* lived some of those same emotions you feel you dare not describe in someone else.

Accept the dare. Step up to the challenge. You owe it to yourself at least to try. For if any character — however far removed from your life and lifestyle — demands that his or her story be told through you, then you must trust that all you need lies within you.

Of course, research may be required. Remember, though, that even in a documentary script, it's the emotions that will touch people, that will affect them, that will move them to deeper places within themselves. And we all — whoever we are — draw from the same pool of emotions.

If you can give yourself permission to tap into that pool within you, you will always write what you know.

The only knowledge that is unique to you is the knowledge of your heart, the wisdom of your soul, the force of your passion. Write from those places that no one else can and you will touch people in ways that no one else can.

Go ahead and write what you know...if you dare.

TRY THIS

On the Muse Stream, write an autobiographical monologue, using any or all of these opening phrases:

- I know terror...

- I know humiliation...

- I know betrayal...

- I know what it feels like to be different...

- I know what it feels like to feel trapped...

- I know what it feels like to be judged...

- I know what it feels like to judge...

Write what you know, from your heart. Surrender to that knowingness and unleash the emotions, passion and truth of your soul onto the page.

TRY THIS TOO

Take one or more of your monologues from the previous exercise and turn it into a scene involving two or more characters. Channel all the emotional truth of your monologue into this interaction.

WRITE TO DISCOVER WHAT YOU KNOW

When we dare to tap into deep, inner places of emotional truth in our writing, what comes out can startle us. More often than is comfortable, it can also force us to reexamine who we are, how we live and our place in the world, and to do it through a more sharply focused lens than we have ever done before.

"Most writers write to say something about other people — and it doesn't last," Gloria Steinem writes in *Revolution from Within*. "Good writers write to find out about themselves, and it lasts forever."

Write what you know, then let that journey carry you to all the places within that you didn't know you knew.

Write to *discover* what you know, to discover what you believe, to uncover hidden depths within yourself that only emerge when you take a leap of faith onto the blank page and write freely from your heart.

ASK YOURSELF THESE QUESTIONS

- What would my screenplay reveal to me about *me*, if I let it?

- Where am I hiding behind my words? Where am I hiding from myself? Where am I hiding from others?

- Where am I letting myself shine through my words? For myself and for others?

Rule #8: Strive for Excellence, not Perfection

Whether in writing or in life, many of us are addicted to perfectionism. Being perfect, we believe, guarantees that we will never be criticized, judged, rejected or humiliated. Being perfect means fewer drafts and revisions. Being perfect means instant stardom (and Oscar-dom) as our screenplay is snapped up in a six-figure deal by a major studio as a vehicle for our favorite actor and/or director.

Okay, so a single-draft opus and six-figure deal may not happen...at least not right away. But being perfect is, well, still a good thing to be. Isn't it?

It might be if it were possible. It isn't. No matter how hard you try and how many drafts you churn out, your writing will never achieve perfection. Never.

Not ever.

Your work may be excellent, accomplished, creative and insightful. It may be innovative and compelling, not to mention cinematically brilliant. But perfect? Not possible.

It's not possible because when we translate an idea or concept into language, we're taking something that is infinite (energy) and dynamic (neural impulses) and converting it into something that is finite (language) and static (squiggles on a page). The resulting "translation" can never be more than approximate.

Can you describe the sunset you experienced last night in words that will accurately and precisely convey to me every shade and nuance of what you saw and felt? Can you write dialogue that unequivocally reproduces the emotions you experienced when your child was born?

Of course you can't. Nor would I want you to. As reader I want to be free to have my own experience of your sunset and your character interactions. As actor, director and cinematographer, I will also have my own experience of your words as I interpret them for an audience. As a filmgoer, my experience, again, will not be an exact replica of yours. Until we can somehow link your writer-brain directly to my filmgoer-brain, that translation will remain imprecise and imperfect.

In the end, perfection is not possible in any creative endeavor. It's not possible in any human endeavor. It's just not possible. As Salvador Dali is said to have cautioned, "Have no fear of perfection, you'll never reach it."

If perfection is elusive, excellence is not. Do your best from one draft to the next to translate your vision onto the pages of your screenplay. But don't beat yourself up or trash your script because it isn't perfect. Accept the inherent imperfection that is the perfection of all creative enterprise, and when you have done the best you can, let it go and move on to your next project.

Look for more tools for achieving excellence in Scenes 6, 7 and 11.

Rule #9: Write!

If this seems the most obvious of my rules, it isn't. Not really. It's easy to put writing aside in favor of research. It's even easier to put writing aside while you use outlines, index cards, diagrams, wall charts and other left-brain devices to try to figure out what your screenplay is all about.

There is nothing to figure out. There is nothing to plot. There is nothing to plan. There is only this word...then this one...then this one.

A writer writes. So write. Write the story that is calling to you. Write what comes as it comes. Whatever it is. You will learn all you need to know about your story and its characters through the writing. If you let its sentences and scenes flow freely through you and surrender to it unconditionally, the world of your screenplay will reveal itself to you, effortlessly.

Don't wait to figure out how your screenplay will end. Don't worry about its direction, theme, structure or focus. Don't worry about acts, beats or plot points. Don't worry about what people will think of it, or of you. Don't worry about anything. Set fingers to keyboard and let your story perform its magic on you, without judgment, censorship or second-guessing.

Should its direction change along the way, don't fight it. Surrender to the moment. Surrender to the story in each moment. Your story knows best.

TAKE RISKS

Creative expression is about risk-taking. It's about boarding *Star Trek*'s starship *Enterprise*, taking off for parts unknown and journeying to places where no one before has dared to go.

When you do that, chances are that not everyone is going to like what you have written. Chances are that someone is going to hate what you have written. It's even possible that someone is going to hate you for what you have written.

It's all right to offend people, even as you entertain them. It's all right to push people's buttons, even as you make them laugh or cry. It's all right to take them up to that ledge on which we artists live...and then to give them a gentle nudge.

Art is about pushing boundaries. It's about pushing your boundaries at least as hard and at least as far as you push your audiences' boundaries.

It's about forcing people (including the artists) out of their comfort zones and inciting them to reexamine their beliefs and rediscover who they think they are.

Sometimes, it's about getting people mad at you. Sometimes, it's good to get people mad at you — for them and for you.

"You've got to go out on a limb," humorist Will Rogers is reputed to have said, "because that's where the fruit is."

ASK YOURSELF THESE QUESTIONS

- Where am I going out on a limb and taking risks with my writing?
- Where am I staying on the ground and clinging to the tree trunk to play it safe?
- Where am I willing to get people riled up?
- Where am I holding myself back for fear of being shamed, ridiculed or attacked?

Commit today to taking more risks, to going out on a limb. Commit today to letting yourself be judged...and letting it be okay.

Rule #10: Respect Every Word and Draft

There is no such thing as a wasted word, line, sentence, scrap of dialogue or screenplay draft. Every word, line, sentence, scrap of dialogue or draft you commit to the page is part of the creative journey that carries you to the next, to the next one after that and, ultimately, to the final word of your final draft.

Respect every word and every draft. Even that first draft — however messy, muddled and murky it is — deserves your respect. All your drafts do. All your screenplays do. All your creative endeavors do. Even the ones that *seem* to go nowhere. Treat each one with the love and compassion it deserves. Treat yourself with the love and compassion *you* deserve.

It's easy to drift into judgment. It's easy to beat yourself up. Don't do it.

Respect your work. Allow it to grow, change and mature. Allow yourself to grow, change and mature as its creator.

PUZZLES AND PATTERNS

You're convinced that what you have just written is at best self-indulgent, at worst irrelevant. It's okay to think that, as long as you refuse to let those judgmental thoughts stop you from continuing.

I'm not asking you to trust that what you have written is perfect. (It isn't! See Rule #8.) I'm asking you to trust that what you have written forms part of a larger pattern that you will not be able to see until you step back from it — later today, tomorrow, next week, next month or next year. Until you are able to see that pattern, you are in no position to judge anything as wasted or irrelevant.

You open a jigsaw puzzle box and toss its contents onto the floor. All you have is a collection of oddly shaped pieces that seem to go nowhere, connect with nothing — like your thoughts, like your words as you sit down to write, like the first draft of your screenplay. Yet, as you slowly fit two pieces together, then ten, then thirty, a pattern emerges.

In your writing, too, a pattern will emerge. You may not be able to see it today, but it is there.

You don't believe me? Think of all the times that you have looked back on difficult moments in your life only to realize that they formed the building blocks of something you now view as positive.

It's the same with your writing. Always.

ASK YOURSELF THESE QUESTIONS

- Can I trust that there is sense and value to my words, even if it is hidden from me in this moment?

- Can I continue writing through and past my fear and judgment, trusting that every word and draft is my partner and teacher?

Rule #11: Set Yourself Up for Success

Whenever I begin work with a new coaching or mentoring client, I always end our first session with, "How much time can you *realistically* devote to your writing over the next week?" Whatever answer I get, I respond with, "Cut it in half and make that your goal until our next session."

It's human nature to set over-ambitious goals. It's also what we are taught in school and what we are encouraged to do by most writing coaches, books, seminars and workshops. Unfortunately, it's also human nature to judge ourselves as less-than when we don't achieve those goals.

At best, when we miss our target, we hold to the original goal and try again. At worst, we lower our expectations. In neither case do we feel good about what we have accomplished. In both cases, we mourn our inadequacy rather than celebrating whatever it was we managed to write.

Isn't it better to set ourselves a one-scene-a-week goal and get it done, rather than to aim for ten scenes a week and end up having written only one?

You may ask: "If the creative output is the same under both scenarios, what difference does it make?"

The difference is how we feel about what we have accomplished...or not accomplished.

In the first situation, we feel sensational — about ourselves and about our screenplay-in-progress. In the second, we feel discouraged, and our perceived failure could continue to haunt and disable us as we move ahead with our writing project.

Set yourself up for success not for failure by giving yourself ridicu-lously easy goals and meeting them, easily. Then build on that success by gradually increasing your goal. And don't forget to celebrate each success! Too often, we ignore our successes and focus on what we have failed to achieve.

TRY THIS

Have you set yourself an over-ambitious writing goal that you are challenged to meet? It could be a word-count goal, a scene goal or a time goal. Whichever it is, cut it in half...and meet it easily. As you meet it, increase it bit by bit, either from one day to the next or one week to the next.

TRY THIS TOO

Too often, when we reach the end of our writing day, we lament all that we have failed to accomplish. Rarely, do we celebrate what we have achieved.

Tonight as you inventory your day, ignore any goal unreached and all tasks left undone. Instead, run through your day and acknowledge everything you achieved, however seemingly inconsequential.

Don't limit this exercise to your screenwriting projects. Include *everything*.

Continue this inventory — in writing if you can — for at least two weeks. As the days progress, notice how your focus evolves from your perceived failures and not-enoughs toward your real successes and attainments.

At the end of each week, pick your most outstanding accomplishment. *Your* most outstanding accomplishment, however insignificant it might seem to your critical, judgmental mind...or to anyone else. You're not comparing your successes with anyone else's. Nor are you comparing today's with last week's. Whatever it was, find a way to reward yourself for it. It doesn't have to be an extravagant or expensive reward. It could be a massage, a specialty coffee at your favorite café, a book you've long coveted or any acknowledgment that is meaningful to you. Whatever your reward, let it be something special. However you earned it, celebrate it!

TIME TO WRITE

In my *Acts of Surrender* memoir, I tell about a period in my life when I knew I had no choice but to write. Thanks to a personal financial crisis,

I also had a mind-numbing, physically demanding job that forced me awake early in the morning, dropped me into bed early in the evening and left me depleted, even on my days off.

Where would I find the time to write?

"Many job-bound writers wake up at four or five in the morning," I write in *Acts of Surrender*. "Could I do that? I had to be realistic, and honest. I was trying to create a schedule I would stick to, not one that would melt away after a week...or a day. I knew myself. A four-in-the-morning routine wouldn't last. What would, then? After many internal negotiations, I chose to set my alarm fifteen minutes earlier than I needed to. I would stay in bed and write during that time. Fifteen minutes wasn't much, but I had to follow the same advice I gave workshop participants: I had to set myself up for success. That meant establishing goals that I could meet easily and, perhaps, exceed. Setting the bar too high was a recipe for disappointment, failure and giving up. As well, I would take the manuscript to work and try to squeeze in a few minutes more during my breaks. And I would write for longer periods on my days off.

"It worked. Progress was slow at first. But by July, I was finished. After two false starts, the first dating back ten years, I had finally completed a first draft of *The StarQuest*."

Remember: Each word you write is another paving stone on the road to completion, however long it takes to lay it.

Rule #12: Empower Yourself

The world is filled with people ready to tell you what to write, how to write, when to write, even where to write. Often, their advice is well-intentioned: They genuinely want you to succeed. Sometimes, however, that advice has little to do with your best interests — or your screenplay's.

Always listen with an open mind to what others have to say. Even as you do, always listen with an open heart to what *you* know to be true — not from a place of ego stubbornness, but from a place of intuitive inner knowingness. Foster that inner knowingness and cultivate discernment. Trust your intuition. Trust yourself.

At the same time, recognize that filmmaking is a collaborative endeavor. Producers have their own ideas. Directors have their own ideas. Actors have their own ideas. Scripts get changed.

Be open to suggestions. Be open to improvements. Get your ego out of the way and use your discernment to know when to fight, when to negotiate, when to hold your ground and when to give in.

Don't compromise your integrity, but be flexible. Empower yourself.

See "The Critique: Seven Critical Tips" in "Eyes on Your Screenplay" (Scene 12) for more pointers on getting and giving feedback.

Rule #12½: Rules? Oh, Yeah. There Are None.

It's been a long time since Rule #1, so...

Screenwriters are creative artists and creative artists are innovators. Creative artists are trailblazers. Creative artists go where others dare not go.

Write what yearns to be released from you onto the page — not as others have done it in the past...not as others tell you to do it.

Write it as only you, with your unique history, voice and style can do it. Write it as only it can be written

Write it as if there are no rules...because there aren't!

Scene 5.
Screenplay Craft:
Getting Inspired

BILL DONOVAN (FORMER PUBLISHER/EDITOR OF
"CREATIVE SCREENWRITING" MAGAZINE)

Go to the emotional epicenter, where it hurts
most, and write on. If you dare.

RON SHELTON (OSCAR-NOMINATED SCREENWRITER OF
"BULL DURHAM")

I learned a long time ago that I can't write a
screenplay that's not about me.

Now Is the Time...

Without the magic of screenwriting, most of the transcendent and transformative moments we have all experienced in a movie theater, in front of a TV screen or even with our noses pressed to our smartphone or tablet display could not exist. Just about every feature film and television show began life as an idea on paper in script form. And it took a screenwriter like you to kindle the alchemical process that converted that idea from the intangible to the physical, from the imagination to a moving picture.

If you have a story in you (and who doesn't?), now is the time to listen to its call and start freeing it onto the page in screenplay form. That's why you're here, isn't it?

Wait! You say don't have a story? Of course you do. Everyone does. Yours simply hasn't bubbled up into your conscious awareness yet. But it will, if you let it.

It doesn't matter whether or not you know in this moment what your story is about. All that matters is that you dive into it. All that matters is that you launch the creative journey that will liberate it from your conscious or unconscious mind. All that matters is that you write.

Now.

Your Ocean of Stories

You carry an ocean of stories within you, an infinite wellspring of ideas, emotions and exploits that sometimes surface to conscious awareness only in the writing of them.

Like the mightiest of the earth's seas, your storied sea is a place of magic and mystery, danger and delight...a medley of the known and the unexplored, a blend of the murky and the magnificent.

You dive into that ocean when you embark on a screenplay...on any kind of storytelling. And like all the great explorers who have preceded you, you may think you know what you will find on your odyssey. Even as you will surely encounter the expected, this journey into your ocean of stories will often astound you as it reveals treasures you never realized were there. It will also occasionally alarm you as it reveals thoughts and beliefs long ago buried.

Don't let your ocean's uncharted depths frighten you into abandoning the adventure. Dive in. Dive into the dreams. Dive into the nightmares. Dive into the joys. Dive into the terrors. Dive into the ocean of your screenplay.

You will not disappear into that ocean. You will not drown in its waves. Its waters will support you. Its waters will anoint you. And you will emerge from that sacred sea transformed in ways you cannot now imagine.

It is impossible to control the changes that will have their way with you through this ocean crossing, just as it is impossible to control the stories that pass onto the page as you write on the Muse Stream. But in immersing yourself in your sea of stories, you *will* be changed.

Why? The act of telling your stories, of converting your thoughts, feelings and experiences to words on a page, is a revolutionary one. As a screenwriter you must be open to the possibility of those changes, without knowing what they will be or how it will all work out when you first set fingers to keyboard.

All you can do is recognize the truth of this moment, of this sensation, of this story, of this word...and move on to the next from a place of trust.

Trust your stories, and yourself — through each word and each sentence, through each slug line, action paragraph and dialogue fragment — until your screenplay page is alive with the wonder of creation, until you are in awe at the life of your creation.

Your Ocean of Stories:
A Guided Meditation

Allow at least 30 minutes for this meditation and for the writing experience that flows from it.

A professionally recorded meditation similar to this one is available for download or streaming.[1] See "Getting Started" (Scene 1) for details on how to access the recording, as well as for tips on how best to use this book's meditations.

Relax. Allow your breath to slow and deepen, slow and deepen, slow and deepen.

Close your eyes for a moment and picture an ocean. Any ocean. Anywhere. An ocean you have seen or visited, or one that resides only in your imagination, only in your heart.

Whichever it is, see that ocean stretching out to the horizon, seemingly limitless in its scope. Feel its infinite nature, its infinite depth, its infinite breadth. Know that every screenplay you have ever written or will write resides in that ocean, just as that ocean resides within you. Know that every screenplay you have ever written or will write is as real and alive now as the sea life that thrives deep below the ocean surface of your imagining.

See yourself now in a boat on that ocean. Open ocean. A large boat or small. It doesn't matter as long as you feel safe, as long as you're comfortable, as long as it's your boat.

Get a sense of that boat that now carries you, supports you, propels you forward.

Feel the salt spray on your face. Feel the gentle swell of the ocean's ebb and flow.

---

[1] Search the relevant site/store for "Mark David Gerson ocean of stories"

Ebb and *flow*...

        Ebb and *flow*...

                Ebb and *flow*...

Allow your breathing to align with that ebb and flow as you become one with this environment you are creating. This ocean. This boat. This sea of stories that stretches as far as the eye can see.

Farther.

If your boat is moving, allow it now to slow or stop. Anywhere. Anywhere at all. As long as you remain in open waters. Drop anchor or allow yourself to drift. It doesn't matter.

Now, in your hands is a net, a special net that scoops up not fish but stories, the stories from which screenplays are born. Stories from the vast undersea world that is the infinite reservoir of your creativity.

Take a deep breath now and cast your net into this sea of your creativity, this sea of your stories, this sea of screenplay-potential. Cast your net and let it fall where it falls, sinking wherever it sinks.

Take a few more breaths, allowing your net to settle. As your net sinks and settles, take a few more breaths, in and out, your breath following the ocean's swell. In and out. In and out. In and out.

Now it's time to raise your net. So do it. Raise your net and see what you have retrieved. What you have received.

Whatever it is is perfect. Perhaps what has emerged makes sense as a story, as a possible story for film, as a potential screenplay. Perhaps it makes no sense to your conscious mind. It doesn't matter. Whatever it is is perfect in this moment. For this moment.

What have you retrieved from the ocean of story? From the depths of your creative waters?

See it. Feel it. Sense it.

Know it. Fully.

And now, write it.

Relish the Chaos

First drafts are messy. First drafts are chaotic. First drafts are disordered. First drafts are inconsistent. First drafts are meandering. First drafts are repetitive. First drafts are too long, or too short. First drafts are a formatting disaster. That's why they are *first* drafts.

First drafts are journeys of discovery. In your first draft, you find out what your story is and what it's about. You learn who your characters are. You meet up with ideas, beliefs and convictions you never knew you had. You come face-to-face with shadow selves that have more than likely long resided hidden within you.

Your first draft is that unplanned drive into the country, that map-free journey alive with synchronicity, serendipity and surprise. Your first draft is where you first taste the magic of the visual potential of the written word. Your first draft is where you experience the alchemy of creation. Your first draft is where you let the story and its characters reveal to you what and who they are, which may resemble nothing that you expected. Your first draft is your first experience of surrender, where you begin to discover that you don't own the story, where you begin to discover that the story owns you.

Don't go into the first draft of your screenplay expecting it to be your final draft. Neither draft will ever be perfect, but your first won't even be excellent. It might not even be good. It might, in fact, be really, really, really bad. Let it be that. Let it be what it is: an exploration...a journey...a voyage into the unknown. Let your screenplay's first draft be your act of surrender to your Muse. And let it, along with every draft up to your final draft, be the perfectly imperfect expression of a transcendent vision that is uniquely yours.

Sixty Story-Starters

If you're not sure how to launch your screenplay, if you have already begun and find yourself stuck, or if you simply need a quick exercise to stir up your creative juices, pick a word or phrase at random from one of the lists on the next pages and use it as a writing prompt. The first list focuses on screenplay action and slug lines; the second, on dialogue.

Remember to write on the Muse Stream — without stopping, thinking or censoring. Let the words, sentences and scenes emerge naturally, and don't worry about how, where or whether they will fit into your final screenplay. Some will, others won't. Your job right now is not to figure anything out. Your job is to write.

Feel free to play with the lists to make them more relevant or challenging: Add, modify or combine phrases, switch genders/tenses, change punctuation, alter a slug line's place and/or time of day, turn positive statements into negatives or negatives into positives, or use a scene description as a dialogue-starter, or vice-versa. At the same time, know that it doesn't matter which you choose because whenever you surrender to the Muse Stream, the perfect words always emerge, regardless of how you begin.

Creativity is about having fun. Think screen*play*. So have fun!

LIGHTS, CAMERA...ACTION!

1. She rummages…

2. A police officer…

3. Laughter, confusion and…

4. A middle-aged couple…

5.   Two boys kick…

6.   EXT. ENCHANTED CASTLE - DAY

7.   An airplane…

8.   The waiter pours out a brandy.

9.   Booming thunder.

10. The soldier raises his arm to salute but…

11. Buster opens the door.

12. Dawning light reveals…

13. Violent spasms shudder through…

14. INT. RICK'S CAFE - NIGHT

15. She stares into the fire.

16. Charlie kicks violently at the snowman.

17. A white-gloved thumb and forefinger gingerly turn the dial on the wall safe.

18. The doorman whistles for a cab…

19. Franklin lifts the pen, hesitates.

20. The phone rings.

21. Yank jerks awake.

22. She hurls her cellphone into the river.

23. INT. KLM TICKET COUNTER - LAX - DAY

24. The FedEx driver presses the doorbell. The chime echoing from inside the house seems to go on forever.

25. Midnight. The restaurant is nearly empty.

26. Snatches of landscape waft in and out of view.

27. The butler glides into the library, unnoticed by the duelers.

28. The neon sign flickers weakly.

29. EXT. EIFFEL TOWER - PARIS, LAS VEGAS - DAY

30. Francie, 55 but trying to look 30, with bottle-blonde hair and heavy makeup.

SAY WHAT?

31. I've died three times, you know.

32. Can you keep a secret?

33. When I stepped off the plane, I...

34. Let's have sex.

35. I wish I remembered....

36. Don't let him take the chicken into bed with him again.

37. I hate clowns.

38. Hide!

39. If I hadn't been born...

40. The day I lost/found...

41. Chocolate?

42. Do you remember...?

43. You forgot the horses.

44. Get me another martini. Make it two.

45. You'll have to come with me.

46. I hate birthdays. Don't you?

47. The day I didn't get married, I...

48. Is it not a fact that...?

49. The fire tells me...

50. I was so scared.

51. Nothing was ever the same after…

52. What do you want me to do about it?

53. Rosebud? Not Rosebud!

54. It was the strangest dream.

55. You're the one making a mistake.

56. I can't be your friend.

57. When I looked into the ant hole, I saw.

58. Unicorns? What do you mean, unicorns?

59. It is the key to everything.

60. The end.

The Spirit of Your Story, the Essence of Your Screenplay: A Guided Meditation

Allow at least 35 minutes for this meditation and for the writing experience that flows from it

Get comfortable and close your eyes. Take a deep breath in, and let it go. Take another. Let that go. As you breathe in and out, let your shoulders drop and feel the muscles in your arms and neck relax. Feel your whole body relax.

With each inhalation, breathe in more deeply and feel yourself breathing in to the essence of this screenplay you are working on, to the essence of your creativity, to the essence of your creative power, to the powerful essence of you.

And with each exhalation, feel more and more of the tension dissolve from your body. Feel all the anxiety dissolve from your body. Feel all the emotional strain and stress dissolve from your body. Let your shoulders drop some more, and feel nothing but peace and calm envelope you.

Be in the moment with that peace. Be in the moment with your breath. Be one with your breath, so that the only thing you are aware of in this instant *is* this instant...is the essence of this instant and, within that essence, the essence of your story, a story that has called to you so strongly for so long...a story whose call you have now, finally, answered.

What is this story? It is the story in screenplay form that you are now writing or will soon be writing. It is the finished story that already exists whole and complete in its own invisible realm, that is already playing out on some other-dimensional movie screen. It is the completed screenplay that is waiting for you to engage with it, that is waiting for you to trust it. That is waiting for you to surrender to it.

So acknowledge that your story knows itself better than you do, that your screenplay knows itself better than you ever will. Acknowledge that and open to all that the story behind your screenplay and the screenplay that expresses your story have to offer you now through this experience.

Continue to focus on your breath. Continue to go deep within. And as you do, as you let your breath carry you deep into your heart and deep in the heart of your story, allow an image, any image, to bubble up into your conscious awareness, an image that represents the energy of your story, the energy of your screenplay.

Don't expect this image to be a literal cinematic representation of your script. It could be, but the probability is high that it won't be. This image need not make conventional sense. There's a good chance that it won't. The image could be a thing. It could be a color. It could be a person. It could be an animal. It could be a sound. It could simply be a feeling.

Whatever it is, let it bubble up into your awareness. Don't judge it. Don't censor it. Just let it emerge and, whatever it is, be okay with it.

Be aware, too, that if this is a repeat meditative experience with the same story and screenplay, a different image may emerge for you now than emerged for you last time. That's okay. Go with whatever bubbles up for you today, with whatever is bubbling up for you right now.

We are dealing with a nonphysical energy and with your mind's representation of that energy. We are also dealing with your evolving relationship with your screenplay, with your story. It's natural for your imagery to evolve as well.

Trust today's representation of that energy. Trust tomorrow's, too, if it shows up differently. Trust that whatever emerges whenever it emerges is perfect for who you are in the moment you intuit and discern it.

Now, before you begin to converse or connect with that image, if you haven't already, begin to get a sensory sense of it. Begin to use your senses to help you connect more fully and deeply with that essence, with that energy — with the essence and energy of your story and your screenplay — through the image that has emerged for you today.

Get a sense of color, if there's color. Get a sense of shape, if there's shape. Get a sense of depth, if there's depth. Get a sense of texture, if there's texture.

Which other of your senses is awakened by it? Smell? Taste? Sound? Music, perhaps? Emotions?

Not all your physical and emotional senses may apply to this image, but they may. Or those that are not relevant today may be relevant on another day, or in a different, perhaps unconventional way.

So, what does this image look like to you right now, even as you know that it could change in the next moment? What does it feel like? If it feels powerful, don't let yourself feel overwhelmed by that power. Know that that power is you, and that that power is an expression not only of the screenplay's essence but of your essence.

Whatever this image is, however you perceive it, whatever its qualities and characteristics, embrace it. Take it in. Breathe it in. Fully. And let your sensory and emotional experience of this image connect you more intimately than ever before with the energy and essence of the story that it represents.

It is time now to listen, to listen to that image, whatever it is. It is time to listen from a deep place deep within you, to listen with your heart to what your screenplay, through this image, has to tell you. You might not hear a conscious message, but something will move through you, however unconsciously. Trust that. And trust that however you experience it is the right and perfect way for you right now.

So take a few moments now to listen...

Now that you have heard, felt or sensed whatever you have heard, felt or sensed, it's time to ask a question of your story, of your screenplay, through the intermediary of this image. So silently ask a question. Then silently listen for an answer.

You may hear your answer. You may sense your answer. You may get nothing clear or obvious. Even if your question seems unanswered in this moment, an answer will come in another moment, likely in an unexpected way in an unexpected moment. Trust that.

Ask another question, and wait for another answer.

And another.

Before we complete this experience, your screenplay has some reassurance to offer you. Listen for it, and hear or feel it in whatever way you hear or feel that.

Finally, let your screenplay offer you some closing words, whatever those words might be today, to help you move forward on the next step of your creative journey with it. Listen for those.

Remember that you have been chosen to bring this story into the physical in the form of a written screenplay. However that may feel on some days, it is one of the greatest gifts of your life. Be with that for a moment or two. And feel what that feels like.

Now, once again, be conscious of your breath. Be conscious too that this process will not end when you open your eyes, but that the intuitive sensings and messages will continue in the hours, days and weeks ahead. Remain open to them. Remain available to them. Trust them.

Be aware now of your physical body, of the physical space you now occupy, as you let your breath return you to full awareness. And when you feel ready, taking all the time you need, gently open your eyes and be fully present, ready to jot down any notes or thoughts from this meditative journey you have just traveled.

Scene 6.
Screenplay Craft:
Getting into
Character

LAWRENCE BLOCK (EDGAR AWARD-WINNING NOVELIST)

In all of my writing, the most effective dialogue
has been that which my characters supplied
themselves.

ELIZABETH BOWEN (NOVELIST & THE ROYAL SOCIETY
OF LITERATURE'S "COMPANION OF LITERATURE")

Characters are not created by writers. They pre-
exist and have to be found.

Whose Story Is It?

A few years ago, I was listening to a guest speaker; let's call him Frank. Frank was sharing his views on the optimal way to develop fictional characters

"In the first half of your story," he counseled the room full of writers, "let your characters do what they want. But when you get to the second half, you have to rein them in."

Frank was adamant, and it took all the self-control I possessed to rein myself in...not because of the first half of his statement, but because of the second.

I was reminded of that story some months later when I began working with Karen, then a new coaching client. Karen had written a powerful memoir, so powerful that it had been nominated for a literary award. Now, a fictional character had accosted her in a misty Irish glen and was insisting that she write his story.

"I don't know how," she moaned.

"You don't have to know how," I replied. "All you have to do is write his memoir."

You see, whatever fictional story we're telling and in whatever medium we're telling it — be it as a novel, short story, stage play or screenplay — we're writing someone's story.

Let me say that again: What we're doing is writing *their* story. And what we often discover in our first draft is not only what that story is but who that character is...who all the characters are who make up that world.

Frank's point was that we spend the first half of our story discovering who the character is. From there, we spend the rest of the story ensuring that our character hews to that portrait.

My point is that we may only know half the truth of who that character is by our story's midpoint. We may discover the whole truth of who she is and what she is about only by writing through to the end.

Why stifle the creative process just when we have finally surrendered to the story's unfoldment? Why limit ourselves and our characters by insisting that at a certain point in our screenplay draft, character and story are fixed for all time?

When I was writing my original screenplay for *The SunQuest*, I had a fairly clear sense of how my antagonist would meet his downfall. At least, I thought I did.

However, as I approached the climax of this final story in what was then known as *The Q'ntana Trilogy*[1], something unanticipated happened: Instead of being conventionally defeated, the villain had a profoundly redemptive experience, transforming him from the ugly adversary of all three stories into a positive force for continuing good.

I was stunned...and scared. Scared because until that moment, I had viewed this character as unremittingly evil and had portrayed him accordingly. Was this sudden (to me) transformation supported by what I had already written? More important, was it supported by the ways I had portrayed him in the first two *Q'ntana* stories? I knew I could revise *The SunQuest* to ensure that his character arc made sense. But *The MoonQuest* and *StarQuest* books were already published; no changes were possible there.

In that moment, I had two choices: I could follow Frank's advice and refuse my villain his redemption, or I could surrender to the higher imperative of both character and story and give myself over to the magic. I chose the latter, and not only because I believe my stories and their characters are smarter than I am (which was proven when I revisited *The MoonQuest* and *StarQuest* and discovered that nothing in those stories threatened the character evolution unfolding in *The SunQuest*). I also made that choice because this character's transformation supported what I had begun to recognize as one of the series' central themes and achieved it in ways that I would have been hard-pressed to consciously manufacture.

Another example: In *The MoonQuest* much about the character O'ric shifted — not only through the first draft, but through many of the drafts. He shifted not because I couldn't reign him in. He shifted because, through the writing, I began to grasp more clearly who he was and to understand his significance to the story.

Rule #10 in my "12½ 'Rules' for Developing Your Characters" in the

---

[1] "There's always more to every story," one of the characters insists in *The MoonQuest*. Apparently, that's true, which is why *The Q'ntana Trilogy* is now *The Legend of Q'ntana*; you can't have a four-part (or more) trilogy!

next chapter reads "How did John become Judy?" Often, characters in our screenplays want to undergo radical changes through the course of that first draft; sometimes in a subsequent draft as well. That's not a bad thing. However, too often we follow Frank's advice and refuse them that freedom, thus stunting their potential...and the story's.

I say give your characters absolute freedom through the entire first draft of your screenplay and, if necessary, beyond. Let your characters be as inconsistent and mercurial as they want to be. Let them veer off in completely senseless directions partway, if that is what they choose. Let your villains become heroes and your heroes become villains. Let them change names, physical characteristics, motivations and story-significance. Let them change gender. Let them change species. Let them change screenplays.

Only by allowing them that unconditional freedom in your first draft can you learn who they truly are and can you be true to their story. After all, it is their story you are telling.

Let the first draft of your screenplay be that imperfect, somewhat muddled journey of discovery — of your characters and of their story. You might, as I did in *The SunQuest*, discover something of major significance about an important character only on the final pages of the draft. That's okay. Use your next draft to bring consistency to the characters you now know more fully. Or you might discover, as I did with my *Q'ntana* antagonist, that you wrote the character consistently without realizing it, and few if any alterations are needed.

Remember whose story you are telling...and get out of the way.

ASK YOURSELF THESE QUESTIONS

- How can I better trust my characters and their stories to reveal themselves to me? Can I do it in *their* time, not mine?
- How can I stop trying to control my screenplays into perfection and instead let them emerge organically?
- How can I better surrender to the magic out of which all creativity is birthed?
- How can I trust that my stories and characters know themselves better than I do?
- How can I let myself be surprised — by my characters and by their stories?

12½ "Rules" for Developing Your Characters

Let these 12½ rules guide and direct you as you free your characters into their story and free their story onto the page — always remembering the first and most important rule of all, which is...

1. THERE ARE NO RULES

How can there be rules when you are dealing with human beings? Any attempt to "build" characters according to an instruction manual will result in cardboard cutouts instead of fully formed, three-dimensional individuals, with all their inconsistencies, paradoxes and eccentricities. Your characters are real people, not manufactured creations. Treat them that way.

2. YOUR CHARACTERS ARE PEOPLE...EVEN THE NONHUMAN ONES

Storytelling is an expression of the human condition. It doesn't matter whether your character is a robot (*Star Wars*' C-3PO), a frog (*The Muppets*' Kermit), a sea sponge (Sponge Bob) or a Klingon (*Star Trek*). You are still writing for human beings about human emotion, and your viewers will only identify with your characters if they recognize some aspect of themselves in those characters.

Let your characters, whatever their species, be that same strange brew of grace and ghastly, saint and sinner, magic and muggle, clarity and confusion, lost and liberated that you are...that we all are. Let your characters live. Let your characters be human.

3. YOUR CHARACTERS AREN'T LOGICAL

Human beings are a mass of contradiction and paradox and are never consistently logical. Even *Star Trek*'s humanoid Vulcans aren't inherently logical. What Vulcans are doing is trying to control or suppress their innate emotions and replace them with logic.

The Vulcan dilemma — the constant struggle between emotion and logic — reminds us that inner conflict is the key to all great characters. We all carry irreconcilable goals, personality aspects and beliefs. Let those intrinsic inner conflicts express through your characters' words, actions and interactions to make them credible.

4. BEING GOD DOESN'T PUT YOU IN CHARGE

God said, "Let there be light," and there was light. Your act of character-creation is like God's in Genesis: an act of allowance, of letting, of surrender.

Surrender to the story that calls to be written. Surrender to how it calls to be written. Surrender to the lives your characters choose to live...for if you're writing a screenplay, those lives are your story.

Just as the Creator in most faith traditions allows you the free will to live your imperative and forge your story through the living of it, your call as story-Creator is to allow the beings who leap from your heart, mind and vision that same freedom.

Gently guide when necessary, but allow them — and yourself — to experience their story as it writes itself onto the page.

Your job as screenwriter-Creator is to let your characters and their story emerge from the formless void and to breathe life into them so that they — and you — can experience all they have come onto your page to live.

5. MAKE FRIENDS WITH YOUR CHARACTERS

Remember your imaginary playmates from childhood? Let your characters be those playmates now. Make friends with them. Spend time with them. Take them on drives. Go for walks with them. Take them to your favorite movies, restaurants, cafes. Then let them take you to theirs...and to their other favorite places, even the unsavory ones. Let them talk to you — not as characters but as people...as friends, if possible. Let them open up to you and share with you who they are and why they are as they are. Let them reveal not only the story that will end up on the page, but the stories behind that story. Let them share with you how and why they think they are misunderstood. Let them share their dreams and secrets, their mistakes and embarrassments. Let them be real.

6. ALL CHARACTERS ARE EXHIBITIONISTS

Your characters long to reveal their lives to you. After all, they chose you to tell their story. Free them to be the exhibitionists they are. Use the "Getting into Character" meditation later in this section if you need help making contact.

7. TRUST YOUR CHARACTERS

You are writing your characters' story, not yours. Trust them to know it better than you ever will. Listen to what they tell you, even when you know they are lying. Let them surprise you. Let them surprise themselves.

8. LOOK AT YOUR CHARACTERS SIDEWAYS

Write a scene that explores a character from the point of view of someone not in the story, someone fictional or real. For example, how would your mother interact with this character? Or your bother? Or your neighbor? Or write a scene or monologue that explores a character from the point of view of a pet or of an inanimate object. How would your character's dog or cat interact with the character or describe the character? What about their house? Their car?

9. BE SPECIFIC...BUT NOT TOO SPECIFIC

Specifics bring us more fully into a character's inner and outer life. Use all your senses — spiritual, visionary and intuitive as well as physical — as you explore, discover and reveal who they are. Let specifics emerge naturally and organically. Provide enough script detail to intrigue a potential actor, without over-defining the role.

10. HOW DID JOHN BECOME JUDY?

As I point out in "Whose Story Is It?", your characters deserve absolute freedom through your first draft, and sometimes beyond, to morph at will — even if that alters significant details about them. Where necessary, use later drafts to bring consistency to the characters and their world.

11. RESPECT EVOLUTION

In most stories, the main character is not the same by the end as she or he was at the beginning. Your responsibility is to portray that evolution, or character arc, in a way that's credible, engaging and entertaining. Remember that your character knows himself better than you do. Listen to what she tells you about her story, about her evolution. Listen to what he tells you about his journey, about his growth. Don't force evolution on your character. Allow it to find its way into your early drafts spontaneously; strengthen it in subsequent drafts.

12. RELAX

Let your exploration of your characters be a joyful journey of discovery. Don't overanalyze your characters, don't obsess about them and don't feel as though you must know everything about them before you can start writing. Begin your story and let the characters reveal themselves to you in the writing, especially in that first draft. Let the process be an organic one not a compulsive one.

12½. THERE ARE NO RULES

Let your characters be whatever *they* are, in all their wondrous and maddening humanness and humanity (even if they're not human!).

Know Your Characters

Discover as much as you can about your characters. Although most of what you learn will never find its way into your screenplay — and some of it should not — exploring the people who populate your story will always enrich your writing.

Even as you must avoid too-specifically detailing your character's physical attributes in the script (it can limit casting options), you can still carry your own idea of what a character looks like.

But looks aren't everything. Know not only your characters' vital statistics but their secrets and dreams. Know not only the color of their eyes but the quality of the fire behind those eyes. Know what happened in their lives before their recorded story begins. Know what shaped them, what excites them, what scares them. Know them as well as you know yourself (better, perhaps), and in that knowing they will leap off the page and onto the screen with full humanity.

As you explore your characters, use all your senses and employ all your curiosity. Keep your mind and heart open to all you perceive and receive, particularly anything that shocks, frightens, irritates or embarrasses them...or you. Through your discernment, you will know what feels right, what feels true. Go with that, not with what your second-thoughts censor would have you do. Let your people speak to you. For only then can they speak to your initial readers and then to your actors, directors and ultimate audiences.

Here are seven tips to help you deepen your knowledge of the people whose stories you are telling.

1. VISUALIZATION

Close your eyes and relax. Envision yourself in a safe, creative place and let your character or characters take shape. Have them guide you through their day, their home, their life. Notice how they dress, how they wear their hair, how they walk, how they talk. Let them show you who they are and how they live. Let them show you who they were and where they came from. Let them show you who they will be and how they expect to get there. Watch them relate to others. See them experience joy. Eavesdrop on them in an intimate moment, an embarrassing moment, a shameful moment. Witness their response to a crisis. Allow your explorations to reveal the unseen as well as the seen, the unsavory as well as the attractive. For additional depth, visit immediately before or immediately after a scene in your screenplay or immediately before or after the time frame of your story.

For a more guided experience, go to the "Getting into Character" guided meditation later in this section.

2. DIALOGUE

With paper and pen or keyboard and screen at hand, get into a meditative space and enter into a written conversation with your character. Ask questions...and wait for answers. Let your characters tell you who, what and why they are. Let them tell you how they are feeling and why.

In early drafts of my *Q'ntana* stories, there were characters who either didn't feel fully formed or who I felt were withholding information from me. I dialogued with each in turn and discovered things I hadn't known, including certain things I wished I didn't have to know. From those dialogues I fleshed out existing scenes and shaped new ones — all of which proved integral to the story.

3. IMAGERY

Give your senses free rein. Ask not only what your character looks like, but what he sounds like, what she smells like, what his skin feels like. If your character were a taste or a flavor, what would that be? If your character were an animal or a bird, which animal or bird would she be? If he were a color or shape, which would he be? If she were a city or country or landscape, which would she be? If he were a particular kind of weather, what would that weather be?

Remember, too, to use your intuitive and visionary abilities — we all have them — to tune in to the story of his life, and the life of her story... to tune in to her spirit and his essence.

4. STOP, LOOK, LISTEN

Watch the people around you. What you can discern about them and about their lives from simple actions, behaviors and physical characteristics? Note how they sit, stand and walk, how they hold themselves. Be aware how they relate to others. Notice not only what they're wearing but how they're wearing it. Pay attention to what is being revealed; pay more attention to what might be being concealed.

See also "The Seven Be's of Effective Film Dialogue," later in this section.

5. THE VIEW FROM INSIDE

Do what actors do as they prepare for a role: Get *inside* your characters in any way you can. Listen to the music they listen to. Read what they might read. Go where they might go. If you're a man, dress as your male characters might; do the same with your female characters if you're a woman. Or cross-dress, if you're up for it. Think *Tootsie, Mrs. Doubtfire* or *Victor Victoria!*

Write a monologue as your character, on the Muse Stream. To get going, make up your own writing prompt or choose one of these: "My name is..." or "I love to..." or "When I look in the mirror, I see..." or "My dream is..." or "I wish..." or "If only..." Or use a character attribute from the next chapter as your monologue-starter. While this monologue may not appear in your script, it will give you valuable insight into your character's life and psyche.

6. THE VIEW FROM OUTSIDE

Write about your characters from the point of view of others in the script. This can be an effective way to discover how characters relate to their family, friends and environment.

7. I'VE GOT A LITTLE LIST

Create a checklist of character traits, quirks and attributes or use the one that follows in the next chapter. Don't overthink or try to figure what each attribute would be for each character. Rather, get yourself into a meditative zone and intuit the answers, always going with first thoughts.

ASK YOURSELF THESE QUESTIONS

- Which of my characters comes across as flat and one-dimensional, more like a department store mannequin than a person?

- What can I add to the script — in description or in dialogue — that will bring that character to life?

Getting into Character: A List of Attributes

From a place of openness and surrender, run through each attribute in the list and allow your character to tell you how it applies to him or her. Don't think about the answer; let it come naturally, easily, spontaneously. Let the character also show you how these attributes play out in his or her life.

Feel free to revise the list and to adapt it to your own needs, eliminating characteristics that aren't relevant to a particular character and adding others better tailored to your story.

Remember: Most of these attributes will never make it directly into your screenplay. They will, however, inform and enrich your storytelling.

- First word or phrase that leaps to mind as you think of this character
- Nickname
- Age (actual or approximate)
- Age this person acts or wishes s/he were
- Gender; gender identity, if different
- Height / Weight / Body Type / Posture
- Physical disabilities or anything that in any way impedes mobility or speech; attitude toward that disability
- Nationality
- Race
- Complexion
- Hair (color, style, length) / Facial hair

- Eyes (shape, color)
- Quality of vision / Glasses? Contacts?
- Scars / Attitude toward scars
- Unusual physical characteristics
- Gait (how this person walks)
- Voice / Manner (soft? grating? blustery?)
- Favorite expression
- Favorite color
- Unusual traits, mannerisms
- Eccentricities, quirks / Odd habits
- Fears / Phobias / Greatest fear
- Maturity level
- Clothing (style, fabric, age, condition); is this what s/he would prefer to be wearing? If not, what would s/he be wearing?
- Jewelry (style, value)
- Profession / Employment; preferred profession/employment, if different
- Hobbies / Interests / Pastimes
- Schooling
- Unusual skills
- Skills valued by others
- Greatest wish / desire
- Best dream already fulfilled
- Greatest regret
- Worst nightmare
- Favorite foods, drinks / Unusual foods, drinks / How s/he takes coffee, tea or other regular beverage
- Preferred music, reading, art, films, TV, etc.
- Pets
- Sexual orientation; his/her awareness of that orientation; others' awareness of that orientation

- Sexual appetite/activity
- Marital/relationship status
- Relationship with and/or attitude toward men, women, children, pets
- Relationship with and/or attitude toward family, self
- Your off-the-top-of-your-head random thought about this character

Getting into Character: A Guided Meditation

Not every question or suggestion will apply to each character, nor could an experience like this cover every potential detail. As with the list in the previous chapter, ignore what is irrelevant and fill in whichever gaps apply to your story.

Allow at least 35 minutes for this meditation and for the writing experience that flows from it

Close your eyes and get comfortable. Allow your body to relax. Breathe in as deeply as you can and let it go. And again. Breathe in to the sureness of your power and empowerment. Breathe out all fear, all doubt, all judgment. Breathe in to your voice and your creativity. Breathe out anything and everything that is not in alignment with that.

Now, let your shoulders drop and feel all stress and strain drain away from them and from your neck, where we carry so much stress, responsibility and anxiety. Feel the tension around your eyes lighten. Too often, we scrunch our eyes and foreheads, trying to focus, trying to see. You don't have to *try* to see anything. This is an experience in allowing... in allowing the vision to come, in allowing the characters who populate your story to present themselves to you...to reveal themselves to you.

So continue to breathe, to focus on your breath, and let everything else go.

Now, from a deep place within you, invite a character from your story to come into consciousness. If this is your first experience with this meditation, I encourage you to not choose a specific character but to allow the character who chooses him- or herself to come to you. It may or may not be the character you would prefer to talk to in this moment. It doesn't matter. What matters is that you open your heart and mind right now to the character who is ready to speak to you, who is ready to share something of her- or himself with you.

More important than that, as important as that is, I invite you to trust whatever you feel, whatever you sense, whatever you hear, whatever you think you know but are afraid to trust. This is an exercise in many things; it is also an exercise in trust.

And so this individual, whoever she or he is, appears before you in whatever way her or she appears before you.

Because this is a generic meditation, I might pose certain questions during our time together that might seem obvious or that might be irrelevant. Just because they don't apply this time or to this story or character doesn't mean that they won't apply next time. For now, feel free to ignore any question that is not applicable and to replace it with your own.

Be aware too that this individual might not be a person. It could be a pet or other animal. It could even be an inanimate object. It could be a clock, or city or a house. It could be anything at all. Again, be open to it showing up however it shows up and free yourself to have the experience that presents itself.

Let's start with what is most likely obvious: What is this person's name? Is this individual male or female? Does what you see match this person's birth gender? Does it match this person's gender identity?

Be aware that your character might be present in your screenplay at different ages and stages in his or her life. If that's the case, this is one of those ages and stages.

And so at this moment in your screenplay and in your character's life, what is your sense of his or her age? Even if you don't know exactly, guess. Does this person appear to be older or younger than his or her age? Some people look and carry themselves as much older than their chronological age. Sometimes the reverse can be true. This is an opportunity to get a sense of what kind of life this person has lived by the connect or disconnect between chronological age and appearance.

At this stage in your character's life, does he or she have a nickname?

What is your character wearing? Is it typical dress for your character? For your character's age? For your character's gender? For your character's profession? For your character's era? If not, what is the significance of this outfit? And what would she or he normally be wearing at this time? Regardless, what is the quality of the clothes he or she is wearing right now? Are they new? Old? How do they fit? Are they pressed and clean? Or worn? Dirty? Do they suit your character or does she or he seem out-of-place in them?

Once again, you may get answers or no answers to some of these questions. You may see clearly or you may sense or intuit or just "know." It doesn't matter. Your experience, whatever it is, is absolutely right and perfect for this moment and this character.

Look at your character's hair. Is it long or short? Thin? Thick? Coarse or fine? Neat or tousled? What color is it? Or colors? Is the color natural or out of a bottle? Is he or she bald?

Let's focus on your character's eyes for a moment. If you can see their color, what color are they? Even if you can't see it, you may be able to sense it. Are they dark? Light? Are they hooded? Open? What do they reveal? What do they conceal? What do you sense of his or her soul through those eyes?

Now, look around the eyes. Do you see lines of worry? Do you see lines of stress or aging elsewhere on his or her face? Is the face smooth or wrinkled? Tanned and leathery? Or light and porcelain?

Is this character wearing makeup? What kind? What does this character's makeup — the amount, the type, the way it's applied — tell you about her, or him?

If this is a teenage or adult male, does he have facial hair? What kind? Is it trimmed or unkempt? Perhaps this is a woman with facial hair. What is it like?

I asked earlier that you let your shoulders drop. Does your character? Does she seem to carry the weight of the world on her shoulders? Or is he relaxed? Does she stand straight or is she stooped?

Now, look at this person's hands. You can tell a lot about someone from her hands, from his fingernails, from what she is holding, from how he is holding it, from what she is refusing to touch.

Remember that many — most, perhaps — of the things you are discerning, learning and/or discovering through this experience may never end up in your final draft — or even in your first draft. Regardless, they offer you cues and clues as to who this character is...to this character's world...to how the world has shaped this character. As you write your screenplay, this knowledge will inform all the ways you present this character — from description and dialogue to his or her interactions with others and with her or his environment.

Now, this character begins to walk. Be aware of the character's gait. Is it strong and confident? Loping? Limping? Hesitant? Long strides?

Tiny steps? Does she walk with ease? Is he barefoot or wearing shoes? What kind of shoes?

Perhaps she is unable to walk. If so, how does she get around?

Now, it's time to engage with this character. Insert yourself into the scene now playing out in your mind's eye. Go for a walk with your character if that's possible. Sit down over a cup of coffee or a pot of tea. Join her in one of her favorite activities. Let him take you to one of his favorite places. Let him take you to a secret place. Let her take you to a sacred place.

Take a few moments for this encounter to play out, however it plays out. As it does, feel free to ask questions, and be open to whatever answers you hear or sense. Pause the recording now and restart it when you are ready to continue.

Before you and your character part company, consider asking these additional questions. Ask the ones that feel right and relevant to your character, your story and your screenplay. Ignore the ones that feel neither. If different questions occur to you, ask those instead.

- Who is your best friend? Why?
- What is your greatest fear?
- What is or was your greatest joy?
- What is your greatest regret?
- What is your biggest secret?
- What defining event in your life has made you who you are today?
- What do you most hate? Who do you most hate?
- What are you most passionate about?
- What do you most cherish? Who do you most cherish?
- What do you cling to?
- What do you need to jettison from your life?

It is now time to say goodbye to your character. Before you part, though, ask one final question; something you didn't think of before this moment or something you were afraid to ask. Be prepared to be surprised by the answer.

Now, thank this person in whatever way feels appropriate to the situation. Thank your character for his openness to you, for her willingness to share what she has shared of herself and her life.

As you prepare to part, take one last look at this person and notice something you missed earlier. However subtle or obvious, this "something" is significant and tells you something new, something you didn't before realize...something, perhaps, that your character was unwilling to reveal directly.

Now, take your leave from this character and become aware once more of your physical breath and your physical body. Be aware of your hands. Be aware of your feet. Move your head. Yawn, stretching your mouth as wide as you can.

When you feel ready, open your eyes, be fully present with all you saw, felt, sensed and experienced, and jot down any notes from the experience...or write whatever in this moment calls to you to be written.

The Seven Be's of Effective Film Dialogue

As I noted when debunking Myth #8, dialogue is not the only critical component of your screenplay. But it is a crucial one; even silent films used title cards to display snippets of speech considered essential to the story.

Much about what an audience learns about your story and the people who populate it will come from the words you put into a character's mouth. And while the quality of their lines will not be the only determining factor for actors considering your script, it will be an important one.

1. BE INVISIBLE

Effective film dialogue tells story, reveals character and stirs up emotion. But it does so obliquely, invisibly, indirectly. The character isn't always aware of what she is exposing as she speaks; the filmgoer isn't always aware how he is being moved forward into the story as he watches and listens.

2. BE AN IMPRESSIONIST ARTIST

Effective film dialogue is not about long-stretches of expository monologue. Nor is it about overwhelming audiences with excessive information. It is more like an Impressionist painting, sketching in just enough color and detail to enable your viewers to "connect the dots." Effective screenwriters trust their actors to deliver nuance and subtext; effective screenwriters trust their audience to get it.

3. BE LIFELIKE, NOT TRUE-LIFE

Effective film dialogue does not reproduce "real" speech. That's because actual speech is nearly always fragmented and rambling. Record and transcribe an unscripted conversation if you want proof. Film dialogue sounds life*like* but is not *true*-life.

4. BE TRUE TO YOUR CHARACTERS

Effective film dialogue is true to each individual character's rhythm, style, cadence and vocabulary, not to the screenwriter's. Effective dialogue is not clichéd, unless speaking in clichés is a quirk of the character. As you did in "Know Your Characters" and in the "Getting into Character" visualization, spend some meditative time in conversation with your characters. Listen as much to how they speak as to what they say.

5. BE A VOYEUR

Effective film dialogue takes you inside a character's heart and head. Next time you're out, do a little eavesdropping. What can you discern about people, about their lives and about their relationships with others from their language and tone, from their posture, gestures and facial expressions? Pay attention not only to what they are saying but to what they are *not* saying and to what that reveals.

6. BE MUSICAL

Effective film dialogue is more than talk. Effective dialogue is music that helps set the mood, pace and rhythm of each scene and of the movie as a whole. Read your dialogue aloud to get a sense of its tempo and cadence.

7. BE QUIET

Sometimes the most effective dialogue is no dialogue. Don't use dialogue where action is more dynamic. Effective screenwriters trust their actors to communicate with a glance or gesture; effective screenwriters never underestimate their audience's intelligence.

Scene 7.
Screenplay Craft:
Setting the Scene

STEPHEN KING (TWO-TIME PRIMETIME EMMY NOMINEE,
WINNER OF 68 LITERARY AWARDS)

Why worry about the ending anyway? Why be such a
control freak? Sooner or later every story comes
out somewhere.

SYDNEY POLLACK (OSCAR-WINNING DIRECTOR OF "OUT
OF AFRICA")

If you play it safe, I can assure you that you
will never achieve anything interesting.

Scenes and Settings

Avoid exhaustive descriptions of your settings and locations unless explicit details are critical to your story's plot and unfolding. Better to offer a mood and sense of place than the kinds of specifics that risk limiting the freedom of the ultimate film's production and creative teams. Your job is to provide just enough information in as evocative a way as you can so that location scouts with script in hand can scour the globe (or your neighborhood) for appropriate shooting sites, then pass their selections to the director and cinematographer for final vetting.

That doesn't mean that the fine details of your settings and locations have no place in your creative journey. Even if you will never describe a Paris street, Wall Street office or cruise ship stateroom with the exactitude of a novelist, your vision of those locations will infuse your storytelling.

It doesn't matter whether your vision matches that of the director, cinematographer and production designer. What matters is that you have a vision and that your vision is present as you write.

What follows are four tools to help you enrich that vision. For each, start by relaxing and getting into an open, judgment-free, logic-free, meditative state.

For a more guided experience go to the "Setting the Scene" guided meditation, later in this section.

1. VISUALIZATION

Instead of applying your meditative imagination to the people in your story, as you did in "Know Your Characters," apply it to their surroundings. See yourself walking or driving through a scene, floating above it, looking up from beneath it, spying on it from behind a curtained window. How else can you experience it? Note the differences each perspective offers you. Explore not only the seen but the unseen. What lies behind the door that no one in the story ever opens? What is going on around the corner?

2. DIALOGUE

Treat a place in your story as though it were a character and have a conversation with it. Ask it some of the same questions you might ask a character, and don't let your logical mind get in the way of the answer. Let it speak to you either in words or in the feelings you get from it, and let it reveal to you something of its spirit and essence. Alternatively, write a monologue from the place's point of view.

3. IMAGERY

Use all your senses to immerse yourself in your setting. Take both an overview and a detailed perspective, experiencing its component parts with the same eye as you take in the whole. What does a place look like? Sound like? What do you smell? What can you touch? Taste?

Go beyond the physical: What do things remind you of? What feelings does this place evoke in you? In your characters?

Now, cross your senses: Take something you would not normally see, taste, hear, touch or smell and apply those senses to it. If you could taste the sky, what would it taste like? If you could hear the grass, what would it sound like? If you could see the birdsong, what would it look like?

4. OBSERVATION

Leaving your headphones off, go for a walk. Whether it's in the still of nature or the buzzing bustle of a city street, put yourself into a state of heightened awareness. Notice everything — from the skittering ant scuttling across the sidewalk to the whispering leaves atop the tallest tree. Be in the moment with everything you experience, and just as you did in the previous exercise, employ all your senses — visionary as well as physical.

Stepping Into Place: A List of Attributes

Use the following checklist to flesh out your sense of the places that show up in your story, even as such detailed description will rarely make it into your script. Don't overthink or try to figure what each attribute would be for each setting. Rather, get meditative and intuit the answers, trusting your first response. Not every item will apply to every place in your story, nor could any list ever be exhaustive. Use what is relevant and discard the rest. Take notes if you choose, or simply let the list rekindle your imagination.

LOCATION

- General (region, city, town, etc.)
- Specific (neighborhood, street, road, etc.)

PACE OF LIFE

- Hurried / Frenzied? Leisurely / Slow?
- Urban? Rural?

TIME

- Date (specific or approximate)
- Season
- Time / Time of day or night

WEATHER & CLIMATE

- Temperature Aridity / Humidity
- Type/quantity/quality of precipitation, wind, sun, cloud, fog
- Relevant sights, sounds, smells

EXTERIORS — GENERAL TOPOGRAPHY

- Altitude
- Flat? Rolling? Hilly? Mountainous? Rocks, cliffs?
- Barren? Lush?
- Bodies of water: ocean, river, lake, stream, marsh, swamp, puddles
- Relevant sights, colors, sounds, smells, textures

EXTERIORS - IMMEDIATE NATURAL ENVIRONMENT

- Place where the scene takes place
- Neighboring area
- Middle- / Long-distance views
- Trees, flowers, grasses, shrubs, other plants/plantings
- Natural growth? / Planted by humans? When?
- Lushness / Sparseness / Health
- Soil color, type, moisture/dryness
- What is just out of view?
- Relevant sights, colors, sounds, smells, textures

EXTERIORS - BUILT ENVIRONMENT

- Age, condition
- Building/structure where the scene takes place
- Neighboring/nearby structures
- Relationship between structures
- Roads, sidewalks, pavement, paths

- Street architecture (benches, lampposts, trashcans, bus stops, parking meters, fire hydrants, other)
- Signs
- Middle- / Long-distance views
- What is just out of view?
- Relevant colors, sounds, smells, textures

EXTERIORS - VEHICLES

- Cars, motorcycles, bicycles, scooters. Years/models?
- Buses, trucks, vans. Models?
- Farm/industrial vehicles. Models?
- Pushcarts, shopping carts, wheelbarrows
- Baby carriages/strollers
- Animal-drawn vehicles
- Other vehicles
- Age, condition, color
- Visible drivers, passengers
- Relevant sights, colors, sounds, smells, textures

INTERIORS — VEHICLES

- Type
- Relevant features
- Age, colors, condition
- Relevant sights, colors, sounds, smells, textures

INTERIORS — INDOOR ENVIRONMENT

- General look, style, state, condition, age
- Furnishings, floor coverings
- Wall hangings, art, photographs
- Knickknacks, other objects

- Light (quality, source)
- Windows, window coverings
- Plants, flowers (condition?)
- Food, drink
- Electronics (computers, TVs, stereos, game consoles)
- Relevant sights, colors, sounds, smells, textures

INTERIOR — INDOOR CLIMATE

- Comfortable? Uncomfortable? How?
- Aridity / Humidity
- Temperature
- Relevant sights, colors, sounds, smells

PEOPLE

See also "Screenplay Craft: Getting Into Character"

- Ages
- Genders
- General health / condition
- Sizes
- Clothing
- Hair
- Facial expressions, other visible signs of attitude
- Activities

ANIMALS

- Ages
- Genders
- Breeds / Sizes
- General health / condition
- Attitude toward people, other animals

MISCELLANEOUS

- General atmosphere, ambiance
- Normal v. unusual
- Visible v. invisible
- Public v. secret
- Numinous/supernatural/sacred

DOMINANT SENSORY STIMULI

- Sights
- Colors
- Tastes
- Smells
- Sounds
- Textures
- Spirit

SECONDARY & SUBTLE SENSORY STIMULI

- Sights
- Colors
- Tastes
- Smells
- Sounds
- Textures
- Spirit

Setting the Scene:
A Guided Meditation

Let this meditation help reignite your sense of the places in your story. Not every question or suggestion will apply universally, nor could an experience like this cover every type of setting or location. As with the list in the previous chapter, ignore what doesn't apply and fill in whatever is missing.

Allow at least 35 to 40 minutes for this meditation and for the writing experience that flows from it.

Close your eyes, take a few deep breaths in, and let them go. Inhale deeply. Breathe it all out. Feel your shoulders drop with your breath. Feel your whole body relax.

Allow your breath to travel through your body, massaging all those areas that feel any stress, any tension, and let your breath ease all the physical knots and smooth out all the jagged edges of your emotions.

Let your breath carry you deeper now, and deeper still. Let it carry you into the heart of your story, into the heart of your screenplay. Breathe in to it and allow yourself to feel it. Allow yourself to sense it. Allow yourself to be carried to a place within it.

If this is your first time with this meditation, it is best not to choose a specific place but to let a place call you to it. It may or may not be the place and time you would prefer to experience in this moment. It doesn't matter. What matters is that you open to what presents itself to you and that you trust — yourself, your feelings, your sensings and your intuition.

So let yourself be dropped into one of the places where your screenplay is set. A place and a time. Breathe in to that place and time, and take a breath or two to reorient yourself to this new place and time and to engage your senses in whatever now surrounds you.

You could be inside or outside. You could be in the far distant past or more recent past. You could be in the present or the future. It could be day or night; spring, summer, winter or fall. So the first thing to notice is where you are and when you are.

What is this place? We will come back to the specifics of it but for now look around and take in all that you see, hear and smell. An overview. Slowly turn 360 degrees and note anything that is different from what you first saw.

Where are you? When are you? If you can and it's relevant, note the year, month and day. Note the specific time or general time of day. Note the season.

I can't ask you questions that are too specific because the range of possibilities for where you find yourself is too vast. Infinite, even.

But as I ask what I ask, remember to engage *all* your senses. To note what things look like...what things sound like...what things taste like... what things smell like...what things evoke in you. To reach out and experience both touch and texture.

Be specific, naming types, brands, models, styles, colors...noting shapes and sizes. Be aware of the age and condition of what you see. Note what things remind you of, what associations they trigger. Be aware, too, of the quality of what you are seeing, sensing and experiencing. The physical quality, of course. But also the nonphysical, sensing quality.

Remember to cross your senses, imagining what something you wouldn't normally taste might taste like if it had a taste...what something that makes no sound might sound like if it could make a sound... what something invisible to the eye might look like if it made itself visible...what something you can't reach might feel like to the touch.

As always, pay attention to your nonphysical senses. Trust your gut, your instinct, your intuition. Trust your emotional response.

Let's begin with the out-of-doors. If you're inside and you can step outside, do it. If you can't step outside but can look out a window, do that. If neither is possible, intuit answers to my questions.

Now that you have stepped outside, what is the first thing you notice? Is it something you see? Or smell? Or sense? Whatever it is, be with that sensation for a moment and know or discern what that tells you about this place and time.

Get a sense of your surroundings and of the significance of this particular place in your story. Even if your story takes place entirely indoors, the people involved may be affected by what's outside, so look around and take it all in. See what you see. Sense what you sense.

The same is true of the weather. It may not be directly related to the events of your story, but it can set a mood or tone that affects your characters. Take note of it.

Is the weather normal for this season, time, place and situation? If not, why not and in what way? Does it support your characters and the events of their story? Or does it create barriers, delays or challenges. Or does it create openings and opportunities?

What is the weather like? Is it cold? Warm? Dry? Humid? Damp? Sunny?

If it's blue, what shade of blue is the sky? What is the sun like? The clouds? Do their shapes remind you of anything? Or the moon and stars if it's nighttime?

Is it overcast? What's the texture of the sky? Of the clouds? What kinds of clouds are they?

Perhaps it's raining. Or snowing? Hailing? How heavily? How big are the raindrops, snowflakes or hailstones? Is it windy? Stormy? How strong is the wind? What kind of storm is it? What does the air feel like?

What about the light? What is that like? The sun casts a different kind of light at different times of day and in different seasons. The phase of the moon affects the quality and availability of light at night.

Now turn your attention to your surroundings — both the natural and manmade. Note trees, grass, flowers and bushes, both wild and domestic. Note rocks, boulders, mountains and hills. Note buildings and other structures. Note roads, sidewalks or pathways. Be aware of water — everything from puddles through creeks and streams to rivers, lakes and oceans. And be aware of what is on the water and in the water, and what its shoreline is like.

Note sounds. Note smells. Reach out and touch something. What is its texture?

Is there anything you notice that is particularly emblematic of this place?

Are there animals around? Birds? What do they look like? Sound like? Are they healthy and content? Or sickly? How do they relate to this environment? How do they relate to your characters?

What about people? Although we're not focusing on people here, I would still like you to notice what you see and sense of any who might be present and to note what that reveals about this place and time.

Be aware, too, of vehicles and other conveyances. Cars, trucks, buses, bicycles and motorcycles. Strollers, baby carriages, shopping carts and pushcarts. Airplanes, helicopters and hot-air balloons. Drones. Farm equipment and construction equipment. And in less modern settings, carts and carriages pulled or pushed by animals or people.

Note a vehicle's speed. Also note its color, model, age, condition and anything unusual about it, as these things can also reveal information about the character of the driver. The seventy-five-year-old woman racing through town in a fire-engine red Ferrari is likely to bear little resemblance to the seventy-five-year-old woman inching through town in an aging Buick.

Similar differentiations can apply to everything you see — the buildings, the natural environment, the pavement. So, again, remember to put *all* your senses to work, including sound and smell, and be open to what those senses reveal to you of what might be going on, both directly and beneath the surface of this place.

What are you standing on? Grass? A meadow? A road or path? If so, what is the road or path made of? Take a step. What is the sound of your shoe or bare foot on the ground? Every surface will sound different. What does this surface sound like?

Continue to look around and be aware, fully, of all the specifics of color, texture, smell...of things that belong, of things that don't belong. Of things that are natural, of things that are in some way manmade or unnatural. Move around too, if that will reveal more to you.

Look beyond your immediate surroundings to what you see in the middle distance and out to the horizon.

Now step inside and do with the inner space all that you have done with the outside space. Even if your story takes place out-of-doors, enter a nearby structure and practice your en-visioning skills on this new environment.

Where are you? What kind of space is this? What kind and type of structure is it? Residential? Commercial? Industrial? Retail? A garage? Something else?

Is it new? Old? Well-kept? Shabby? Neat? Dirty? Austere and anti-septic? Richly appointed? Comfortable? Utilitarian?

Is it large, spacious and airy? Cramped and tiny? Claustrophobic?

What about windows? Are there windows in this space? If not, what does that feel like? If there are, are they large with expansive views? Or are they small and prison-like? Perhaps they are even barred? Are they clean? Dirty? What do you see out the windows? Can you open one? If so, do any smells waft in?

Notice colors. Smells. Sounds. Shapes. Textures. And light. What is the light like? Is it natural, from a window or skylight? Or artificial? What's the color and quality of the light? Is it direct? Diffuse? Bright? Dim?

What goes on in this space? Is it a residential space? Commercial? Retail? Something else? What is the official function of this particular room or area? The unofficial function? What, in your screenplay, has happened or will happen in this space?

Is the space welcoming? Off-putting?

What kind of furnishings and or fixtures do you see here? Note the style and period. Note age and condition. Are they comfortable? Again, notice colors and textures and what they tell you about this place.

Is anything hanging on the walls? What do they tell you? Are there books, magazines or artwork? Are there movies? Photographs? Plants? Knickknacks? Is there music? Anything unusual? Eccentric? Out-of-the-ordinary? Unexpected?

What about electronics? Is there computer equipment? A television? A telephone? A sound system? A game console? Something else?

Look in closets, cabinets and drawers for more clues to this room's story and history and to the stories and histories of its owners, inhabitants and occupants.

Absorb all that this space has to show you, to share with you. Sights. Sounds. Smells. Tastes. Textures. What do your nonphysical senses tell you of the world of this room?

Now move into adjacent rooms or spaces and engage with them in the same way, using both your senses and your sensings to discover and uncover both the obvious and the subtle, the in-view and the concealed.

Of course, it's not possible to go into every specific of every possibility. So take a few moments to be aware of things that I haven't mentioned, things that are unique to this place and time, things that are especially relevant to your story.

Once again, moving beyond your physical senses, what does this place feel like? What does your gut tell you about it? What does your instinct tell you? Your intuition? What do your emotions tell you about this place?

If this place were a person or an animal, what kind of person or animal would it be? And if this place could speak, what would it say to you right now? What would it choose not to say to you right now?

Before we bring this experience to a close, walk through this place one final time. Step outside again if that feels appropriate. Take a last look around. Notice anything you might have missed previously.

Know that you can return at any time to this place and pick out other things that you missed...pick out new feelings that you are not now aware of. You can come back at a different of time of day, a different season, a different year, a different point in your story. For no place remains the same through time, even through a single day.

You can also come back to this place as an invisible observer of characters in your story, to see how they interact with each other here and to see what this place is to them, means to them, how it treats them, how they treat it. Their relationship with it.

One final experience before you leave: 1 would like you to conjure up in some way the essence of this place. 1 would like you to listen to its wisdom about itself. Let it speak to you, either in words or in the feelings you get from it. Let this place, from its innermost soul, reveal something of itself to you. And as you might do with a person, ask it what it's biggest secret is. Allow yourself to be surprised by the answer.

And now, knowing you can return whenever you choose, bid this place and time a grateful goodbye and allow yourself to begin to feel yourself leaving that place and returning to this one, knowing that all you experienced, whether recorded on paper or not, remains within you, ready to inform, enrich, enhance and infuse your screenplay.

Once more, be aware of your breath and feel your body in this time, in this place. Move your fingers. Move your toes. Move your head. And when you're ready, open your eyes, be present and jot down any notes or details about your experiences that you don't want to forget.

Scene 8. Screenplay Craft: Adapting a Novel

PETER BOGDANOVICH (OSCAR-NOMINATED DIRECTOR & SCREENWRITER OF "THE LAST PICTURE SHOW")

A lot of what I know I learned through osmosis.

ERNEST HEMINGWAY (NOBEL & PULITZER PRIZE-WINNING AUTHOR)

We are all apprentices in a craft where no one ever becomes a master.

Caveat Scriptor!

Always make sure that there are no legal impediments to your screen-play version, even if the novel you want to adapt to film is in the public domain.

Unless you are the novel's author, secure the necessary rights before you start writing. If you don't, chances are your script will never be produced — either because the rights are already spoken for or because the author has no interest in a film adaption.

The Journey from Prose to Script

It's March 1995, a chilly spring morning in rural Nova Scotia. With notepad on my lap, pen in hand and a fire crackling in the Kemac stove, I begin the day's work on my *MoonQuest* novel, grateful that this first draft is nearly finished. To my surprise, what emerges onto the page is not the usual third-person narrative. Instead, I find myself writing in the first person as Toshar, the main character.

It doesn't take me long to realize that Toshar's voice is the story's voice and that I will have to rewrite *The MoonQuest* from scratch, from his perspective. To do it, I know I will have to delete a bunch of scenes, add many new ones and subject those that survive to wholesale revision.

My old editor-self would have approached the task as an exercise in left-brain mechanics. My novice Muse Stream-self recognizes the need for a more right-brain approach.

Instead of forcing *The MoonQuest* into this new, first-person form, I decide to treat the story as its own sentient entity and let it tell me what is necessary and what is expendable. Instead of trying to figure out which scenes to retain and which to cut, I choose to let the story find its own telling.

If my early experiences with *The MoonQuest* helped me to trust in the wisdom of the story, I now allow myself to trust it even more. The result? The rewrite streams out of me with an ease and speed I never expected or could have imagined.

Why am I telling you this story when it has nothing to do with screenwriting? Because more than a decade later, I would use the identical strategy to adapt my *MoonQuest* and *StarQuest* novels into screenplays.

What I'm saying here is that all the key precepts you are encountering in *Organic Screenwriting* apply equally to film adaptations:

- Get out of your own way.

- Silence your critical and judgmental selves.

- Trust that your story is smarter than you are, and surrender to that superior wisdom.

- Listen to your characters: It's their story you are telling.

- Focus on story, not structure.

- Don't worry about beats or plot points.

- Heed the voice of your Muse and your intuition.

- Practice discernment.

- Write on the Muse Stream.

Yes, write on the Muse Stream. Even though you are not writing an original screenplay, the Muse Stream remains your most effective conduit to the story's essence. If you let it, it is that essence that will guide you as you translate the story from one form to another.

Five Top Film-Adaptation Tips

What follows are five basic craft considerations to bear in mind as you read and reread the novel and move forward with your adaptation. Bear them in mind, but don't worry about them as you write. Don't even focus on them. Let them hover on the fringes of your awareness as you listen to the story and as you listen for the story's best expression as a screenplay. Later, when it's time for a new draft, you can add them to your revision checklist.

1. DIALOGUE

Adapting a novel involves more than stripping out all the novel's description and copying-and-pasting its dialogue into Final Draft. Not all the book's dialogue will have a place in the film. Some speeches, for example, may run too long. With others, their point might be more eloquently expressed visually. Talk to your characters and find out from them what is necessary and what is superfluous.

See "Screenplay Craft: Getting Into Character" for more about character and dialogue.

2. NARRATION

In fiction, the presence of a narrator or narrative voice can reveal much to the reader about the story and its characters. Most films have neither a narrator nor a single narrative voice. As screenwriter, you will need to find alternative ways — visually and/or through dialogue — to give viewers the information they need.

3. ACTION AND DESCRIPTION

You have limited space in your screenplay to paint the scenes and settings your novel can do at its leisure. Evocative, concise writing is critical.

4. PLOT AND THEME

Even a simple novel may have multiple themes and subplots. A complex novel will have more. Unless you are writing a modern-day version of Erich von Stroheim's *Greed* (a silent film that clocked in at close to eight hours), you'll have to streamline the story to focus on a core plot and theme. In doing so, you may find yourself eliminating subplots, characters and settings that are superfluous and altering or merging others. Be as ruthless as necessary.

5. THE POWER OF OSMOSIS

One of the best ways to learn how to adapt a novel for the screen is to watch films and read the novels that inspired them — not analytically, but for pleasure.

Osmosis is one of the most powerful learning tools available to the human heart and mind. When we read great writing and watch great films, we absorb the writer's craft and technique; the filmmaker's too. We sense at a deep level what works and what doesn't. Without having to know or understand how or why, without needing to parse or dissect, the power of the words we read and the images we see find their way into our writing.

You won't be copying. You will be absorbing, filtering and adapting. You will be learning — in the easiest and most fun way imaginable: by doing nothing more than enjoying another's creations.

Scene 9.
Cine-Vision

ROBERT TOWNE (OSCAR-WINNING SCREENWRITER OF
"CHINATOWN")

Part of the process of writing is not so much to
explain your vision but to discover it. I think
that's what you do when you write: You find out
what you think.

ORSON WELLES (OSCAR-WINNING SCREENWRITER OF
"CITIZEN KANE")

Learn from your own interior vision of things,
as if there had never been a D.W. Griffith, or an
Eisenstein, or a Ford, or a Renoir, or anybody.

What's Your Vision?

Do you know who you are as a screenwriter? As a writer? Do you have a vision for your writing? For your career? Do you have a vision for the screenplay you're working on? For the screenplay you have barely begun to conceive?

Just as a business crafts a mission statement to bring its goals into focus and to stay aligned with its aim and intention, a writer's vision statement can work similarly.

Holding a vision for yourself as a writer, as well as for an individual screenplay project, can help you more easily move into writing. It can sustain you through the entire process of conception, creation, revision and submission, keeping you aligned with your script's energy, theme, focus, direction and plot. And as I mentioned in "On Screen with the Muse Stream" (Scene 2), it can also help get you back on track if you're feeling stuck.

The vision statements I have created for my writing projects have often served as part of my gear-change from the outer to the inner, from mind-focus to Muse-focus, and have ensured that all I wrote hewed as closely as possible to the story's true essence...and to mine.

A vision statement is not something you think about or plot out. It's something you feel. It can be as brief as a sentence or as long as a page. It can speak in broad terms about your role as screenwriter or in specific terms about a particular screenplay — even if you are not yet clear what it's about.

Nor are vision statements fixed in stone. As your screenplay progresses and as you mature through the writing of it, you may need to refine your vision statement to match new insights and awareness.

Your work with your vision statement doesn't end once you have finished your first draft...or even your final draft. It doesn't end once you have released drafts (or the final script) out into the world.

Reread your vision statement before launching each new draft. Reread it before sharing completed drafts with friends or colleagues.

Hold to your vision when you pitch your idea and submit your screenplay. Hold to your vision when you receive feedback, criticism or reviews — positive or negative. Hold to your vision as you talk about your script with agents, producers, directors and actors. Hold to your vision when agents, producers, directors or actors ask you to make changes or do rewrites.

This vision, as embodied in and by your vision statement, will always keep you centered and aligned with the true heart of your work.

What about loglines? Can a logline stand in for a vision statement?

If you are not yet familiar with loglines, you soon will be: A logline is a one-sentence grabber that both distills your story and sells it. It's a vital arrow in your screenwriter's quiver, a marketing tool that is nearly always required with script submission. If your vision statement is the corporate mission statement we talked about earlier, your logline is the ad slogan that sells one of the corporation's products.

A logline can complement your vision statement by helping to keep you focused on your story as you write. It is not a replacement.

It takes skill and practice to write an effective logline, and you will find scores of books and websites that offer instruction on how to do it.

It takes heart, passion and a sense of purpose to write a vision statement. The "Visioning" exercise and two-part "Vision Quest" meditation later in this section will help you get there. You will find a third approach to creating your vision statement at the end of "Editing from Both Sides of Your Brain" in "The Edit Suite" (Scene 11).

My Vision

I have crafted many vision statements over the years, not only for my writing projects but for my vision of my "writer self." What follows are three examples: for my *Q'ntana* screenplays and novels, for my *Acts of Surrender* memoir and for myself as the writer I am.

MY "LEGEND OF Q'NTANA" STORIES

These stories have always been bigger than me — from the moment the first one insisted itself onto the page.

These are stories that have so long been such a part of my life that it's as though they live deep within my cells.

I am every one of their characters, villain as much as hero, and have lived each of their joys, triumphs, disappointments, betrayals and disasters.

For decades, I have watched their themes play out in the world around me, just as I have experienced them play out in my own life...and not always comfortably. In the end, I am more than the storyteller. I am the story.'

MY "ACTS OF SURRENDER" MEMOIR

Acts of Surrender is an exploration for me and an inspiration for its readers.

It is designed to open readers to the possibilities of freedom in their own lives and to the gifts of surrender.

It's about a life not lived without fear but in spite of fear, a life lived in surrender to a higher imperative, a life lived as the Fool in the tarot lives: in faith, and trusting (not always with evidence) that all is good, all is safe and all is provided for.

As I write, I let my stories reveal their innate teachings through the telling of them.

My job is to keep interpretation to a minimum.

My job is to recount and relate, to reveal and recapitulate, to walk the earth naked once more, clothed only in the truths that have revealed themselves to me through the living of them.

I open my heart to this story, my story, more baldly and boldly told than through any parable, as powerful as such telling can be and is.

I open my heart and reveal my vulnerabilities and fears (and, yes, revel in them) so that others may feel free to reveal, revel in and move through theirs.

Acts of Surrender is about the consciousness of freedom through surrender, awakening and revealing itself in the hearts of all those it touches.

MARK DAVID GERSON: "THE WRITER I AM"

Perhaps the sentences I write are the seams that hold me together. Perhaps, that's the real reason I write. Perhaps, in the end, it's the only reason.

Visioning Your Screenplay

Ask yourself these questions, but don't use your analytical mind to figure out the answers. Instead, use your visionary mind to sense the answers, to feel the answers, to intuit the answers.

- What is my vision for my story?
- What is my vision for my screenplay?
- What is my vision for myself as a screenwriter? For myself as a writer?

Write whatever comes to you, on the Muse Stream. Let it be as long or a short as it needs to be. Don't judge or analyze it. It doesn't have to make sense. Just let it be what it is.

If no answers come right away, don't think or worry about it. Let the questions swirl around inside you as though you are tasting a vintage wine. Let them steep within you as though you are brewing a fine tea. Meditate, go for a walk or do something else unrelated to your screenplay. The answers will come when they are ready. The answers will come when you are ready.

Vision Quest:
A Guided Meditation

Allow at least 45 minutes to complete both parts of this meditation and for the writing exercise that follows each part.

A professionally recorded version of this meditation is available for download or streaming as part of "The Voice of the Muse Companion: Guided Meditations for Writers." It is nearly identical to what follows. See "Getting Started" (Scene 1) for details on how to access the recording, as well as for tips on how best to use this book's meditations.

PART 1: IMAGING YOUR WORK

Relax. Close your eyes. Let your hands fall to your lap if you are sitting, to your abdomen if you are lying down. Breathe...deeply...in and out...in and out...in and out.

Continue to breathe, deeply, and focus on your eyes. If you wear glasses or contacts, imagine for a moment perfect vision without them. Imagine unassisted clarity without correction.

Breathe in to that.

See white light around your eyes and your third eye, that chakra or energy center that lies between your eyebrows and above the bridge of your nose. See that white light cleaning, clearing and cleansing any blurriness, fuzziness, distortion. Feel all veils being pulled away, one by one by one by one. And as each veil dissolves, your vision becomes clearer and clearer and clearer.

Now, without removing all your attention from your eyes, move some of your focus to your heart. Be aware of the veils that surround your heart, whatever form they take. Just be aware of them. Don't judge them.

Now, taking a deep breath, let the outermost veil fall away. Just feel it fall away and dissolve. And when you breathe in again, notice that your heart feels lighter and freer and clearer.

And as you breathe in again, another veil falls away. And another. And another.

Feel how much lighter your heart feels, how much freer your heart feels.

It's okay if it feels a bit scary. Just feel what you feel. Know that you are safe.

Keep breathing and feel yourself grow lighter and freer, lighter and freer, as you move closer to the heart of the matter and closer to who you are as the writer you are.

And what a wondrous place that is.

Once more, breathe in, and if there is another veil there, breathe it away. And the next. And the next. And the next, until all that remains is a brilliant light, no longer veiled and dimmed, in your heart. Breathe in to that and feel it.

Now, let the light from your eyes and the light from your heart connect in a ring of light that circulates energy from eyes to heart and around again. Your vision and your heart as one.

Now, see a second ring of light, moving in the opposite direction from the first, this time connecting your heart to the hands resting on your lap or abdomen. Around and around. A constant and consistent river of radiance.

Connect the two rings and you now have a figure eight or infinity symbol within you, as this inner light arcs from eyes to heart...heart to hands...hands to heart...heart back to eyes. And again. And again. And again, creating an infinite, luminous flow with your heart as its center.

As the energy circulates through that figure eight, be aware of the light pulsing in the topmost tips of your fingers, the hands with which you create, the hands that form part of the channel that brings your worlds into reality. Perhaps you feel the pulsing. Perhaps you don't. Whatever you feel physically, know that the energy is there, the light is there. The creative power is there — in your fingers, in your hands, in your eyes and in your heart, as the flow continues.

Sit with that flow for a few moments, feeling yourself immersed in its river of light and in the creative power that is moving through you.

Now, move your focus away from the infinity symbol and back to your eyes, your heart and your hands. Let a beam of light radiate out from your eyes, another beam of light from your heart and a third beam of light from your hands — all meeting at a point in front of you, in front of your heart.

That point in front of you, connected to you by all that light, by that pyramid or triangle of light is your work as a writer.

Perhaps it's your body of work. Perhaps it's a particular piece of work. Or a single aspect of your work. It doesn't matter. Whatever feels right in this moment, let that be whatever it is in this moment.

So your work stands separate from you but connected to you, in that space where all the beams of light meet just in front of you, in front of your heart. There is your writing.

I'm going to ask you some questions about your writing. I want you to allow the first answer that comes to mind to be the answer. And I want you to know that you will remember it long enough to put it on paper, if that is where it needs to go.

So, focusing the beams of light that travel from your heart, eyes and hands and onto that writing space in front of you...

- If your writing or the particular screenplay you are working on or planning were a color, what color would it be? Just let the color come. Note it. Don't judge or analyze it. Be with it. Know that in this moment, that color represents your writing in general or one specific script. Be with that color for a few breaths.

- Now, your writing or the particular screenplay you are working on or planning is a space, shape or image. What is that space, shape or image? Again, don't judge or analyze. Let it be what it is. See it if you can. Note it. Know that this, too, you will remember long enough to write down or draw, if appropriate.

- Now, your writing or the particular screenplay you are working on or planning is a sound. Music, perhaps. What kind of sound, what kind of music is it for you in this moment? Perhaps it's music that shows up in your screenplay or is in another way directly related to the script. Perhaps not. Whatever the sound or music is, breathe in to it. Be part of it and one with it. Let it surround you and enfold you, filling you with its melodies and harmonies, with its simplicity or complexity. That sound, however it is, whatever it is, is part of you. You will remember that too, when and if it comes time to put it to paper...or to sing it or play it, if that is how you choose to express or experience it.

- Now, use your sense of smell. What does that tell you about your writing? About the particular screenplay you are working on or planning? About who you are as a writer? Is it a sweet smell? A smell that reminds you of something? Again, just be aware of it, and let it be.

- One final physical sense: What would your writing or the particular screenplay you are working on or planning taste like if you could taste it? Perhaps there's a particular food or type of food. Perhaps it's a food that's part of your story or that is directly or indirectly related to your screenplay in another way. What is it? Is it a chocolate sundae, rich and creamy? Comfort food? Maybe it's fresh, baked bread. Maybe it's a juicy pineapple. Maybe it's sweet and flowing like honey. Maybe it's spicy. Tangy. Tart. Let it be what it is. Acknowledge it. Be with it.

Now, go deeper still and let one word emerge that captures the spirit and essence of your work or this particular screenplay. Let it be the first word that comes, whatever it is. Don't judge it, don't analyze it. Don't second-guess. If it makes no sense to your conscious mind, perhaps that's just as well. Let it be.

Now, staying in this meditative space that you're in, pause the recording and jot down some notes about what you experienced — the color, the smell, the taste, the shape, the word...particularly the word.

Or take the word that just came to you and write on the Muse Stream from the phrase, "My writing <or the name of your screenplay> is <your word>..."

When you're finished, don't read what you have written. Instead, restart the recording, close your eyes and continue.

PART 2: YOUR VISION

Reconnect with that energy, that space. With that triangle, that pyramid of light. Again, begin to feel the light connecting your eyes and heart and hands with your work, your work as the writer you are, the screenwriter you are.

Now that you have experienced your writing from each of your senses, move your directed focus away from those specific senses.

Stand above them. Get an overview of all that you experienced, all the different connections you felt with your writing through sensing your writing.

From that vantage point, look down at that space in front of you where you and your writing come together, and breathe into that space for a few breaths.

Feel the fullness of it and the vastness of it. The specifics of it too. Feel all of it. Be all of it. Know all of it for the first time, again.

Feel, too, your connection with that part of you that is the screenwriter and the screenwriting and the screenplay. Feel it and breathe into it. Breathe deeply into it.

Now, answer these questions...

- What is it that, deep inside of you, you want to convey through your writing? First answer. No thinking about it. Let the answer come freely.

- What is it you want people to experience through your writing? Again, go with whatever comes up first. Don't censor. Don't judge.

- What do you want people to experience of you through your writing?

- What do you want people to experience of themselves through your writing?

Open your eyes, again pause the recording and jot down your answers to some of those questions, to whichever questions were answered. Remember not to judge or analyze. Just record your experiences, the answers you've received.

Stay in a meditative space, and when you're done restart the recording.

Now, turn to a fresh sheet of paper or to a fresh page in your writing app. At the top of the page, write: "I, *<your name>*, am a screenwriter. Through my writing *<or the name of your screenplay>*, I..."

From that opening, write on the Muse Stream, letting what follows be as long or as short as it needs to be.

When you're done, sit quietly in the energy of that for a few minutes before reading it aloud. Feel free to revisit and revise this statement or series of statements as you, your project and your writing mature.

Scene 10. Taming Your Inner Film Critic

DAVID BRIND (SCREENWRITER)

You have to stay true to the voice, to what it is
that distinguishes you as a writer.

CATHERINE JOHNSON (BAFTA-NOMINATED
SCREENWRITER OF "MAMA MIA")

The most common mistakes new playwrights make is
to impose self-limitations. Be bold.

After You've Written

The first thing most of us want to do after having written is to read over what we have written. And our first impulse as we read it, especially if we have never written on the Muse Stream before, is to judge it. Harshly.

There are reasons for that.

When you write a screenplay without thinking, without editing, without stopping, your formatting can be inconsistent, incorrect or even in chaos. That can true, too, of your dialogue, your descriptions and your characterization. Even of your theme and plot. It may feel as though your entire screenplay is little more than a jumbled, disordered mess.

More than that, your language can seem unrefined and your emotions unfamiliar. It may seem as though the writer's voice you have known until this moment is absent, usurped by something alien, something disturbing. It may seem as though the thoughts and beliefs you have known until this moment may be absent, usurped by ones you could never imagine yourself holding.

What you write from the deep, heartful place to which your Muse Stream carries you can be raw, can seem foreign, can be markedly different from anything you have ever written before.

It's natural to leap to judgment. That place of judgment serves neither you nor your work.

Chances are, judgment will convince you to do one of two things: Abandon your screenplay or hack at it mercilessly.

Here's how to do it differently. After you've written, ask yourself these questions before looking at your screenplay:

- Do I feel able to read my words from an openhearted place of non-judgment? Of objective discernment?

- Can I give myself permission to read it at least one time through without changing anything?

- Do I feel able to partner with my story rather than control it? Do I feel able to surrender to its wisdom?

- Can I give myself permission to read from a place of respect and compassion, for the screenplay and for myself? From a place of trust in my innate creativity? In my Muse? In the essence of the screenplay itself?

Unless you can answer yes, unequivocally, to all these questions, let your work sit unread until you can. Unless you can answer yes, you risk damaging both your creation and your creativity by reading what you have written. Unless you can answer yes, it is premature to do anything with what you have written other than set it aside and write something else. It is certainly premature to consider doing any editing work on it.

When you can answer yes, remember Screenwriting Rule #10 and read with respect — for your work and for yourself.

Taming Your Critic:
A Guided Meditation

Allow at least 30 minutes for this meditation and for the writing experience that flows from it.

A professionally recorded meditation similar to this one is available for download or streaming.[1] See "Getting Started" (Scene 1) for details on how to access the recording, as well as for tips on how best to use this book's meditations.

Sit or lie down in a comfortable position. Close your eyes and take a few deep breaths. Let yourself relax. Feel yourself relax on your breath.

Now, let your shoulders drop...and drop some more. And some more. And some more. Breathe deeply and fully, feeling the breath fill not only your lungs and abdomen but your entire body — from head to toes and back again.

And again. And again.

Feel the breath cleanse you. Feel it dissolve your fears, your anxiety, your stress. Feel it strengthen you, empower you. Feel it protect you, keep you safe. Feel it open your heart. Feel it open your mind.

There have been times in your life when you have been criticized, times in your life when you have been judged. Of course there have. We have all had those experiences. As children. As adolescents. As adults.

Sometimes, the experience rolled off us painlessly. Sometimes, it felt excruciatingly cruel. Sometimes, we forged ahead in spite of it. Sometimes, it shut us down.

It's all normal, all perfect, all part of the human experience. And as with all human experience, we can choose how to react or respond, we can choose how each instance will affect us.

---

[1] Search the relevant site/store for "Mark David Gerson "taming your critic"

Don't judge how you have reacted or responded in the past. Simply be aware and keep breathing. Fully. Deeply. Allow your breath to once again dissolve any stress or anxiety triggered by unpleasant memories.

Know that you are safe. Protected. Free from harm of any sort.

From that place of relaxed breathing, from that place of safety, call into your mind, heart and/or consciousness your harshest critic. Perhaps it's someone in your past or present life. A teacher. A parent. A sibling. Another relative. A friend. A school or neighborhood bully. A producer, director, actor or fellow writer. A day-job colleague, boss or coworker.

Feel whatever charge you feel around this individual, and breathe. Feel whatever charge you feel around this individual and let that feeling dissolve on your breath.

Now, let that critic transform into some kind of image, something that represents that critic, that stands in for that critic. A symbol. A metaphor. Perhaps it's an animal. Perhaps it's a color or shape. Perhaps it's a snake or serpent. Perhaps it's another human form or another type of form altogether. Or perhaps it doesn't change form at all.

Let it be what it is and know that however it shows up is perfect for you in this moment. Regardless of how it shows up, see it not as an external critic but as an internalized aspect of you, ready to engage with you.

Whatever it is, whoever it is, however it is, greet it and begin a dialogue with it. Have a conversation with it. Engage with it.

Either write this dialogue as it occurs or let it emerge silently in your heart.

In the first part of your conversation, ask your critic why it judged you so cruelly, what provoked its behavior, what it was afraid of.

If this is an ongoing situation, frame your questions in the present tense.

Listen with an open heart. Respond with an open heart. Allow compassion. Allow understanding. Allow forgiveness. Allow love.

Give yourself thirty seconds of clock time for this part of the experience. Or pause the recording until you are ready to continue.

Be aware that if you are experiencing judgment, there are probably areas in your life where you are expressing judgment. Have compassion for yourself for *your* judgments. Be understanding. Be forgiving. Be loving. Be open. Be respectful. Toward yourself.

Commit as well to directing those same attitudes toward others, toward anyone you are tempted to criticize harshly.

Now, as you return to the conversation with your critic, ask it how the two of you can work together from this moment forward to bring your work, your writing and your life to its fullest, most magnificent potential.

Converse. Discuss. Negotiate. Dialogue. Engage. Silently or in writing.

Again, be loving and compassionate. Be understanding and forgiving. Be respectful. Be open.

Allow another thirty seconds of clock time for this part of the experience. Or, again, pause the recording until you feel ready to continue.

Now it's time to bring your encounter to a close. Thank this aspect of yourself for its assistance, for its openness, for its willingness to transform. And commit to this new partnership. Commit, too, to the spirit of cooperation the two of you have just forged in love and mutual respect.

When you're done, write of your experiences and discoveries. Use all your senses to paint a picture in words of your new awareness and your renewed creative power.

When you're finished writing, remember to read your words from a place of love, openness and non-judgment. Remember, too, your commitment to partnership and cooperation.

Still feeling judgmental? Return to the "Let Judgment Go" at the end of "Thirteen Creativity-Killing Myths About Screenwriting" (Scene 3).

Scene 11.
The Edit Suite

MICHAEL J. FOX (EMMY- & GOLDEN GLOBE-WINNING
ACTOR)

I am careful not to confuse excellence with
perfection. Excellence I can reach for; perfection
is God's business.

DAVID S. WARD (OSCAR-WINNING SCREENWRITER OF
"THE STING")

I don't think that there's such a thing as a
perfect script.

Why Edit?

No matter how good the first draft of your screenplay is, I guarantee that it isn't ready to be pitched. It probably isn't ready to be shown to a spouse, partner or screenwriting colleague either.

Every first draft needs editing. Every second draft also needs editing. Third and fourth drafts too.

Why?

As you rewrite, edit and revise, you ensure that...

- Your dialogue is compelling and that it moves your story forward

- Your description and action paragraphs are evocative and concise

- Your characters are convincing and that their journey (character arc) is credible

- Each scene builds on the last, that each scene moves the story forward and that all your scenes come together to create an engrossing story that builds to a compelling climax and a satisfying conclusion

- Your screenplay aligns with your vision statement

You also work to...

- Eliminate redundancy and ensure consistency

- Fix typos, correct spelling, tidy up grammar and punctuation

- Make sure your screenplay is properly formatted

In short, each draft of your screenplay further refines the raw clay of your idea into the masterful script it deserves to be and readies it to be pitched or produced.

How many drafts do you need?

As many as it takes to get your screenplay as good as you can make it. It could take five drafts or fifty. Each script is unique and each comes with its own set of challenges, regardless of your experience and skill level.

Here's the good news: Your screenplay doesn't have to be perfect. In fact, it can't be perfect because perfection doesn't exist.

Excellence, however, does. But it takes meticulous, painstaking and committed editing to get there — whether you're Ingmar Bergman, Francis Ford Coppola or Jane or John Screenwriter. If you want readers to keep turning the pages of your screenplay — and you need readers to like it if it's ever going to progress to development and production — you must edit it through multiple drafts and revisions. As many it takes.

Just so you know, unless you're producing the ultimate film yourself, your final draft will not be *the* final draft. Agents, producers, directors and even actors may insist on yet more changes before agreeing to take it on.

So don't send your screenplay out into the world quite yet. Read on and let this section guide you through a singular revision process that is certain to make your script more attractive to those whose decisions will determine its fate...and yours.

Editing from Both Sides of Your Brain

When we think about editing, we generally view it as a left-brain undertaking, a mental activity that is largely about precision and fine detail. We also tend to describe it with harsh, aggressive language that's almost abusive. The screenwriter, in this conventional view of the process, must always be in charge...must never relinquish control. For example, we talk about *forcing* the script to our will, about *hacking away* at our writing and about *hammering* our screenplay into shape, and we argue that we must *rein in* our characters or, worse still, *gag* or *restrain* them. Language like that disrespects not only our screenplay but ourselves as its creator.

I prefer to take a whole-brain approach to editing, one that marries left-brain detail with right-brain intuition and discernment. It's a radical paradigm that views the editing process as one of "re-Vision," of revisiting your original vision for your screenplay and putting all your heart, art, craft and skill into aligning what's on your computer screen with that vision.

As you edit, revise and rewrite your script, see yourself as a jeweler, delicately etching your rough stone into the jewel that reflects the vision your heart has conceived and received, then lovingly polishing it until you achieve the look and texture you desire.

Your vision is the light force of your screenplay, the life force of your screenplay. It is the spirit that is its essence, the breath that keeps it alive. Your vision is your dream for your screenplay, the expression of your intention. It is what guides it, drives it and propels it — from conception to completion and if you're lucky, up onto the big screen..

The more deeply you stay connected to that vision, however broadly or specifically you have drawn it, the more completely your finished script will remain true to that life force, that dream, that intention. And the truer you will be to the story that called upon you to commit it to the page and breathe life into it.

TRY THIS

As I pointed out in "Cine-Vision," working with a vision statement is a powerful way to stay aligned with your screenplay — all the way through your revisions to your final draft. If you haven't yet created a vision statement, now would be a good time to do so.

Your vision statement can be as simple as getting into a meditative space and writing on the Muse Stream from the phrase, "My vision for *<title of screenplay>* is..." or "My screenplay's vision for me is..."

Alternatively, allow your work to speak about itself, writing on the Muse Stream from a phrase like, "I am *<title of screenplay>*. I am about..." Or use either the "Visioning Your Screenplay" exercise or the "Vision Quest" meditations in the "Cine-Vision" section to guide you.

Whatever your choice, allow to come whatever comes, whether it speaks in metaphor, in general terms or with the most specific of detail. The length doesn't matter. The form and language don't matter. Your conscious mind's understanding of what you have written doesn't matter.

What matters is that at some level you and your creation sing the same song and that that harmony supports you not only as you write but as you refine and enrich your original draft and all the drafts that follow.

12½ Secrets to Whole-Brain Editing

1. BE TRUE TO YOUR VISION

Before you launch into your screenplay's first revision and any subsequent draft, revisit your vision statement. Don't merely read it. Feel it. Embody it. Connect with it, and through it connect with the essence of your work. If possible, read your vision statement aloud — with heart, power, confidence and intent. Thus empowered, the words of your vision statement will fuel and inspire you as you move through each draft and each revision.

2. TAKE YOUR TIME

There's no rush. Let your work sit quietly for a time before you launch into revision — especially if you are feeling hypercritical and can't help but judge what you have written. That time could be a day, a week, a month or six months after you complete a draft. And it could be longer or shorter from one draft of your screenplay to the next.

Even if an agent or producer is pressuring you to finish, don't panic. Remember that your story deserves you at your best and that your director, actors and audience deserve no less. So give both yourself and your script the space and distance that allow you to approach your revisions heartfully, objectively and discerningly.

3. USE YOUR WHOLE BRAIN

Don't rely solely on the logical, detail-oriented side of your brain when you edit your screenplay. Using your whole brain and body will allow you to see beyond obvious errors and to correct more than surface issues.

Does a line of dialogue not feel right? Does some elusive something about one of your characters feel "off" in some way that you can't identify? Is there a scene or part of a scene that feels as though it doesn't belong? Do you have a nagging sensation that something key is missing from your plot? Does something else feel out of whack?

Trust those feelings, whether they pop into your head or you feel them somewhere in your body. The more you do, the more those intuitive sensings will alert you to problems in your screenplay and the more clearly they will offer you solutions.

As you become more adept as a screenwriter, more in tune with your screenplay and its vision, and more in touch with your Muse, you will gain an easy, innate knowingness of what works in your script and what doesn't, without always being able to articulate why. That sixth sense will also direct you to the appropriate fix or improvement — again, often without explanation. Your intuition will never lead you astray. It is the voice of your vision and the voice of screenplay.

4. TALK TO YOUR SCREENPLAY

As I wrote in Rule #2 back in "12½ 'Rules' for Writing Your Screenplay" (Scene 4), your screenplay knows itself, its story and its imperative better than you do. Listen for its voice and let it tell you where the problems are in your script. Listen with your heart and trust what you hear — in terms of plot, characters, dialogue, settings, theme or anything else.

Remember: Your story knows best — about every aspect of your screenplay and at every stage of the process. The more you "consult" it, the easier your revision journey will be and the truer to your vision your final screenplay will be.

For help connecting with the voice of your screenplay, revisit "The Spirit of Your Story, the Essence of Your Screenplay" in "Screenplay Craft: Inspiration" (Scene 5).

5. TALK TO YOUR CHARACTERS

Just as your story is smarter than you are, your characters know their story better than you do. Talk to your characters. Let them tell you what needs to be told and what doesn't. Let them tell you how it needs to be told. Let them tell you what is missing or superfluous. Let them tell you what's not right about *their* story. Let them guide you.

Need help? Revisit the exercises and meditation in "Screenplay Craft: Getting Into Character" (Scene 6).

6. READ ALOUD

We are always more attuned to the rhythm and flow of our language when we read aloud. We often read more thoroughly when we read aloud. You will want to read your dialogue aloud, of course. But read your action paragraphs aloud as well. In both instances, your voice will help alert you to where you have strayed off course.

As much as you will discover what works and what doesn't when you read aloud, you will learn even more when your dialogue and action are acted out. Befriend actors or look for other opportunities to get your script "performed." Record the reading sessions where possible. Or record yourself reading your script. Listen at least once to the playback with your eyes closed to better imagine how what you are hearing will look on screen.

7. ACCEPT THAT LANGUAGE IS NOT PERFECT

As you revise, never hesitate to seek out more forceful and evocative ways to translate your vision onto the page. Be aware, though, that translation is an art and that language can rarely more than approximate emotion and experience. Picture an evocative scene you hope to include in your screenplay and imagine trying to recreate that in words. You can come close. Yet whatever your mastery of the language, you will not recreate every nuance of your vision, emotion and experience. That's okay. Accept the creative perfection of that innate imperfection and...

8. DO YOUR BEST

Do your best to write the dialogue and paint the scenes that most accurately reflect your story. Do your best to commit your vision to paper. Do your best to polish, enhance and enliven your screenplay so that it aligns with that vision. Do your best with each draft and when it's time, declare it finished and let it go.

9. SUSPEND JUDGMENT

Judgment is a blunt instrument. Discernment is a more delicate tool: a marriage of intellect and intuition, heart and mind. Heartful revision is about discernment, not judgment. We all judge ourselves and our work too harshly at times. Notice your judgment but don't give in to it. And don't let it get in the way of your editing.

Feeling judgmental? Revisiting these two meditations will help you edit with more clarity and less judgment:

- "Let Judgment Go" ("Thirteen Creativity-Killing Myths About Screenwriting," Scene 3)
- "Taming Your Critic" ("Taming Your Inner Film Critic," Scene 10).

As I mentioned above in "#2. Take Your Time," delay your revision work until you feel able to read your screenplay from a place of wisdom and perception, not from one of self-criticism and self-doubt.

10. RESPECT ALL YOUR DRAFTS

Revision is not about taking a broadax to your screenplay. It's about treating each draft as a necessary stage in its growth toward maturity. Just as you gently, sometimes firmly, guide your children toward the fulfillment of their unique destinies, guide your screenplay with that same spirit of respect — for yourself as its creator as well as for your creation, which has its own vision and imperative.

No word you write is ever wasted. Each scene you craft, even if it ends up on your cutting room floor, has value. Every word and scene is an integral step on the journey toward a completed draft, and each draft is key to the journey toward a completed screenplay...and film.

Allow your work to grow, change and mature, and...

11. BE THE WRITER YOU ARE

Each draft of your screenplay will teach you, and from each draft and screenplay you will mature in your art and your craft. Strive for excellence, which is achievable, not for perfection, which is not. Be the writer you are.

12. DON'T OBSESS

Through every stage of your experience with your screenplay, there will be infinite opportunities for you to obsess about one aspect or another of the process. Don't do it.

12½. BE TRUE TO YOUR VISION

Hold your vision in your heart and mind as you revise, and do your best to align all your edits and rewrites with that vision.

12½ "Rules" for Editing Your Screenplay the Whole-Brain Way

1. THERE ARE NO RULES

Of course, there aren't. There never are. In revision as in writing, there is no single right way to edit your screenplay that is guaranteed to work for you every time. There is only the way that works for you *today*. I emphasize "today" because what works for you in revising one script or draft may not always work on the next. So be open, be flexible and remember to use your whole brain as you edit.

2. BE TRUE TO YOUR CHARACTERS

Are your characters telling their story rather than allowing it to unfold through their words and actions? Your characters are people, not mouthpieces. Make sure you have given them scenes and situations that reveal their story...and the dialogue to go with it.

Does the dialogue you have written reflect the age, gender, nationality, education level and quirks of the character speaking it? Or does it sound too much like every other character? Or too much like you? Make sure your characters' language, rhythm, style and vocabulary express who they are and make sure that what appears on the page reveals that identity to your audience. Remember Secret #6 from "12½ Secrets to Whole-Brain Editing"? One of the best ways to test your dialogue is to read it aloud. Record it and play it back to get a better sense of its authenticity. Better yet, get actor friends to act it out for you.

3. WATCH YOUR LANGUAGE

As I noted when busting Myth #9, evocative language is key to your screenplay's success. It will not only engage and captivate your first readers, the ones who will decide the fate of your script, it will kindle the imagination of the creative team whose job it will be to turn your words into moving pictures. Here are a few ways to strengthen your language.

- *Employ Forceful Nouns and Verbs.* Adjectives and adverbs are too often little more than crutches propping up weak nouns and verbs. Find high-octane nouns and verbs that stand on their own power and kick away those crutches. Even when adverbs and adjectives help you paint a more expressive picture, seek out forceful nouns and verbs to accompany them for more potent writing. Not all adjectives and adverbs are superfluous, of course. Here as everywhere, use your discernment. If you need help...

- *Make Friends with a Thesaurus.* Use it (in revision, *not* in writing) to replace adjectives with robust nouns and adverbs with dynamic verbs. Use it, too, to find adverbs and adjectives that more eloquently and effectively reflect your intent. As with any friendship, don't abuse your relationship with your thesaurus. Use it as a tool, not as a crutch.

- *Convert Those Clichés.* Clichéd writing is lazy writing. Clichéd writing is impotent writing. Clichéd writing is dull. Replace platitudes, hackneyed phrases and overused metaphors with original writing that provokes, astounds and astonishes. If you need help, consult a thesaurus.

- *Get Active (Unless You Need to Be Passive).* When you write with the active voice, the subject of the sentence performs the action: "The dog [the subject] bit Tommy." In action paragraphs, the active voice is simpler and easier to read than is the passive voice; it's also more direct, impactful and, according to studies, more memorable. Perhaps even more important in page-limited screenplays, the active voice is more concise. (See Rule #4.) With the passive voice, the subject *receives* the action: "Tommy was bitten by the dog." The passive voice can be vague, awkward, stilted and wordy. These are called "action paragraphs" for a reason!

What about dialogue? The same guidelines apply *unless* a character's journey, age, gender, nationality, education level, quirks and/or inherent speech patterns demand something different. Remember Rule #2 and be true to your characters.

4. COMPRESS, COMPRESS, COMPRESS

Whether in dialogue or action, get to the heart of the matter in as few lines as necessary, without compromising your story or its characters.

- Are there words, phrases, sentences, characters or scenes that detract from the essence of your story, that weaken your theme, that overcomplicate your plot, that overexplain a motivation or situation, that fail to illuminate your vision? Either delete them or rework them so that they strengthen your story and your vision.

- Have you used two or three words or sentences — or scenes — where one would do? Find ways to say more with less.

- Have you used four- or five-syllable words when words of one or two syllables would work as well? Be simple. Be direct. In simplicity lies power.

- Are your action paragraphs written in the passive voice? Revisit Rule #3 and get active!

- Have you filled a scene with dialogue where action — or a look — would convey character and/or move the story forward more effectively or eloquently? Rewrite the scene to delete unnecessary dialogue.

- Don't have characters call each other by name, unless it serves a particular purpose. Notice how rarely you do that when you're in conversation.

- In your action paragraphs, look for empty words like "very," "really" and "quite." More often than not, they are really quite unnecessary. When they appear in dialogue, do they reveal character or move the story forward? If not, consider cutting them.

Practice your compression skills by revisiting the paragraph-tightening exercise at the end of Myth #9.

5. ELIMINATE SUPERFLUOUS SPECIFICS

Have you described characters in a way that limits casting options? Have you described a place or object in more detail than is needed to support the story you're telling? As important as evocative language is, don't use it to over-describe the people, places and objects of your story. Give your director, production designer, cinematographer, location manager, casting director and actors enough detail to evoke your vision but not so much that it limits their imagination and cripples their ability to marry your vision to theirs as they bring your words to life on the screen.

For example, consider describing the mood a place kindles rather than going into descriptive specifics. When it comes to characters, offer an age range and suggest a type — "vain," "headstrong," "walks as though he's carrying a great weight" or "is the sort of person who always drives under the speed limit," for example — rather than being overly detailed in your description. Give no more than the story requires and make sure your dialogue supports it.

With both action and dialogue, consider using imagery to evoke character and settings. Liken your character to a particular animal, food, car, tree or landscape. Equate your setting with a type of weather or person or emotion. Engage your reader's senses using not only physical senses of smell, taste, texture and sound but spiritual senses and feelings. Types of music or particular songs can also offer a potent metaphoric suggestions. As with everything else, don't overdo it.

6. CLEAR UP INCONSISTENCIES AND REDUNDANCIES

Are slug lines that represent the same location not set up identically throughout your script? Are place and character names spelled differently in different scenes? Have you unintentionally given a character duplicate lines of dialogue? Have you unintentionally given the same lines of dialogue to two characters?

Inconsistencies and redundancies like these can easily creep into your screenplay, especially when you are writing rapidly on the Muse Stream. They can also be easy to miss, especially after multiple drafts and readings.

As you are nearing your final draft, devote at least one read-through to bringing consistency to your screenplay and another to deleting unnecessary repetition.

7. SET YOUR FAVORITES FREE

The character you love most, the description you consider unparalleled, the piece of dialogue you cannot bear to cut, the scene you believe to be beyond brilliant, the subplot you think is super-clever: These are your favorites, and you may have to let some of them go.

View each one objectively, from a place of loving detachment. Look at each in light of your vision. Ask your character whether these lines, scenes and/or subplots serve his or her story. Ask your story whether they belong in the screenplay or whether they are distractions. Unless they serve the story, file them for later use in this or another work, be it a future script or another piece of writing.

Do you have an unhealthy attachment to certain characters? Ask yourself some of those same questions.

8. TRUST YOUR ACTORS AND DIRECTOR

Your screenplay is only one step on your story's journey to the screen. Actors will make the characters their own. The director, cinematographer and production designer will do likewise.

- Don't direct the film from the pages of your script: Remove all camera direction and delete all unnecessary stage direction.

- Delete anything that gets in the way of an actor's interpretation of a character, including "wrylies," those parenthetical dialogue directions that indicate the mood, tone or attitude you want an actor to assume. The only exception would be where a line of dialogue could be interpreted multiple ways; where possible or appropriate in those situations, rewrite the line for clarity.

9. TRUST YOUR AUDIENCE

What have you overexplained? Where is dialogue superfluous? Trust your audience to be able to follow your story without needing to be spoon-fed.

10. DON'T CHEAT YOUR AUDIENCE

What have you failed to show or explain? Are there gaps in your storyline that will leave your audience confused? Are there holes in your character arc that will make your characters less human...less credible? Ask yourself the questions your audience will — and make sure your script answers them.

11. YOU ARE CERTAIN TO MAKE CHANGES YOU WILL REGRET

It's easy, during revision, to make changes in one draft that you regret in the next. To avoid losing your pre-corrected text, create a new document and printout for each draft. If you must make changes within a particular draft, keep the original text visible by enclosing your change in square brackets or by displaying it in a different font or color.

If your screenwriting application allows you to revert to a previous draft, enable that feature. And if you have access to a backup system or service that potentially saves multiple versions of a document, like Apple's Time Machine or the Backblaze backup service, use it to retain access to those earlier drafts.

12. MEET INDUSTRY STANDARDS

Now is the time to make sure that your script...

- Adheres to standard screenplay format
- Does not exceed 120 pages
- Contains no camera directions
- Contains no stage direction or actor direction
- Does not include endless paragraphs of dialogue not broken up by action paragraphs...or endless paragraphs of action unbroken by dialogue

There may be no rules for screen*writing*, but there are for submitting screen*plays*. Make sure your script meets industry standards.

12½. THERE ARE NO RULES

Every aspect of your screenwriting process, including editing, is a creative act. And creativity is about innovation, free-thinking, breaking new ground and breaking old rules. Find your own way...in your first draft and in all your drafts.

Scene 12.
Eyes on Your
Screenplay

WILLIAM GOLDMAN (OSCAR-WINNING SCREENWRITER OF
"ALL THE PRESIDENT'S MEN" & "BUTCH CASSIDY AND
THE SUNDANCE KID")
Nobody knows anything.

VIRGINIA WOOLF (NOVELIST & ESSAYIST)
Praise and blame alike mean nothing.

The Critique: Seven Critical Tips

At certain points on your journey with your screenplay, you will want to seek input from friends, family members or writing colleagues. Screenwriting is a solitary pursuit, so it's natural to reach out for feedback. (I prefer the word "feedback" to "critique." It sounds more supportive and less judgmental.)

Feedback can either be helpful or disruptive. It can either foster your creative process or cripple it. It can either match *Roget*'s "sympathetic vibration" synonym or the screeching distortion you get from a malfunctioning sound system.

How do you ensure that others' views and comments support your writing project not distort it? By always following my Seven Be's of Empowered Feedback when you share your work with *anyone*, including with your best friend, your life partner, your writing partner or members of your writers' group.

THE SEVEN BE'S OF EMPOWERED FEEDBACK

1. BE SELECTIVE

Seek out only those people who will support you and your script. Never assume that those closest to you will fall into that category. Often, without intending to hurt you, they are the most critical and least helpful.

When someone asks to read all or part of your screenplay, always use your discernment and give yourself permission to say no, when appropriate. Just because your best friends are actors, directors or screenwriters doesn't make them the best people from whom to seek feedback.

The same applies to writers' groups. Get a sense of the group before joining, and once you are attending, note the type of feedback offered by its members before agreeing to share your work. The only reason to offer feedback is to support the writer and his or her work. Not all groups share that philosophy.

Both "The Voice of the Muse: Answering the Call to Write" and "Writer's Block Unblocked: Seven Surefire Ways to Free Up Your Writing and Creative Flow" offer detailed suggestions on how to set up your own writers' group.

2. BE OPEN

Don't be overprotective and suffocating. Don't let fear hold you back from sharing your work and your vision. Filmmaking is a collaborative process, so it's important to starting letting your screenplay be read by others. As you do, be open to their perceptions and comments. At the same time, exercise discernment in determining which of those perceptions and comments are relevant and which can be dismissed at this moment in your screenplay's development and yours.

3. BE AWARE

To everything there is a season. At different stages in your work and in your creative process, you will be ready to hear different things. Respect where you are and seek only the type and depth of feedback that you are prepared to receive and integrate. Recognize when you are at your most raw and respect that too. As always, discernment is key.

4. BE CLEAR

Be clear within yourself about the type of feedback that you require and desire at this stage on your journey with your screenplay. For example:

- Do you want to know what emotions your work evokes? Whether your reader found one of your scenes funny? Touching? Compelling?

- Do you want to know whether the reader was able to identify with your protagonist? Whether your characters were original and credible? Whether your dialogue was natural or appropriate? Whether your sex scenes or scenes of violence were too graphic? Not graphic enough?

- Do you want detailed line-by-line input? Or are you interested only in general comments?

- Or perhaps you seek nothing more than a pat on the back for having completed a first draft...or simply for having written.

Only you can determine what will support your creative process at this time and what might damage it, so...

5. BE EXPLICIT

Once you have determined the type and depth of feedback that is appropriate for you and your screenplay right now, ask for it — clearly, directly and with neither apology nor equivocation. Your reader cannot know how best to support you unless you make your needs clear.

Don't be shy or embarrassed to make those needs known. If you are vague, hesitant or unclear, you open yourself to comments that you may not be ready to hear, comments that could feel hurtful or damaging, even if they are not intended to be so.

6. BE STRONG

Know what you want and don't be afraid to speak up — lovingly, compassionately and, again, without apology — when you are not getting it, or when you are getting something you didn't ask for. This is *your* screenplay and *your* creative process. You have every right to seek out what will help and support you as you bring your script to completion. In this, you are not only training yourself to determine what will assist you, you are training your friends, family and fellow writers to provide feedback in supportive ways and to seek it for themselves in empowered ways.

7. BE DISCERNING

Deep inside, you know your screenplay's strengths and weaknesses. Tap into that inner knowingness and rely on it to discern which comments it is wisest to ignore and which support you and serve your story.

SEEKING FEEDBACK?
ASK YOURSELF THESE QUESTIONS

- How can I be clearer within myself about the feedback I require right now and with others about the feedback I am seeking?

- How can I be more discerning about where and to whom I turn for feedback?

- How can I be more respectful of my screenplay's needs and my own when seeking feedback?
- How can I be more discriminating in determining which feedback to take to heart and which to dismiss?

OFFERING FEEDBACK?
ASK YOURSELF THESE QUESTIONS

- How can I listen more completely to the nature of the feedback that has been requested of me?
- How can I be clearer and more specific in the feedback I offer?
- How can I be more respectful of the work and its creator, offering feedback that doesn't show how smart I am but instead serves the needs and growth of the screenwriter and his or her work?

Slings and Arrows

Your script will pass through many hands on its way to a producer's "yes" and through many more on its journey to the screen. Through that journey, you are likely to experience much rejection, negativity and criticism. It's unfortunate, but that's the way of the world and the way of the film industry.

It's easy to feel discouraged and destroyed. It's easy to look for unhealthy ways to numb those feelings. It's easy to want to give up.

When that happens, take a moment to go deep within, to that place where the best expression of your story resides, to that place where the committed, passionate and discerning screenwriter you are resides.

Here's where your vision statement — not only for your screenplay but for yourself as the screenwriter you are — can help. How? By reminding you why you wrote what you wrote and by reminding you why it is that you write.

Vision statement or not, know that the words of your screenplay may be an expression of you but they are not you. Know, too, that others' words and actions, whether intentionally cruel or not, have no power to harm or stifle you, unless you allow yourself to be hurt or blocked.

Whatever the fate of your screenplay, take neither praise nor criticism too seriously. Find ways to hold your center through the professional and emotional vicissitudes that are part of every creative artist's life. Remember Rule #12 in "12½ 'Rules' for Writing Your Screenplay" (Scene 4) and empower yourself.

You *Will* Be Rejected

SHAWNEE BARTON (SCREENWRITER)

I received your rejection by email recently, which was surprising since I did not submit an application to the Art San Diego Short Film Program. Like most artists, I am accustomed to having my work rejected, but being rejected from something I did not enter is a new low.[1]

Unlike Shawnee Barton's, most rejections are not unsolicited. At the same time, few are the creative artists who never experience rejection. When someone passes on your screenplay, regardless of the reason, here are six ways to help you get through and past the pain.

1. REAL MEN CRY; REAL WOMEN CRY TOO

Don't bottle up your feelings. And don't get self-destructive. Feel what you feel. All of it. Cry. Curse. Yell. Scream. Throw things. Throw up. Then get past the rejection and move on.

2. WRITE YOUR FEELINGS

Powerful emotions birth powerful writing. Remember Screenwriting Rule #5? Go for your jugular and channel all the ways you are feeling into one of your characters — if not as part of this screenplay, then as part of another one.

You don't have an available story or character and aren't ready to create one? Journal your rage and anguish.

---

[1] "From Insult to Injury: Shawnee Burton on Artist Rejection," by Kathryn Born. Chicago Art Magazine, 2011-08-08 (http://chicagoartmagazine.com/2011/08/from-insult-to-injury-shawnee-barton-on-artist-rejection/)

232 MARK DAVID GERSON

3. TAKE WRITER'S REVENGE

Write a scene where you subject whoever rejected you to something unspeakably hideous, hurtful and horrific. It's the writer's equivalent of sticking pins into a voodoo doll. This scene may never find its way into one of your screenplays, but you'll have more fun writing it than you ever ought to admit!

4. LOOK FOR THE SILVER LINING

It sounds clichéd but it remains true: Every experience, however emotionally debilitating, contains within it the seeds of something positive. You may not be able to see the redemptive value of this rejection today and that's fine. But once the pain has begun to subside, be open to a flash of insight that will reveal the silver lining around your storm cloud of rejection.

5. LOOK FOR THE SPARK OF TRUTH

It doesn't happen often, but your rejection letter could include reasons for the turndown, other than the standard "does not meet our needs at this time." If someone has taken the time to offer feedback, pay attention to it, using the discernment we talked about in "The Critique: Seven Critical Tips" to determine whether it highlights real weaknesses that it would serve you to address in a new draft.

6. KEEP WRITING

Don't let one rejection — or one hundred or one thousand — stop you. Keep writing and keep seeking out ways to become a better writer.

From Spielberg to Tarantino: Tales from the Infamously Rejected

The media world is littered with later-regretted rejections. My favorite story, not because it's the most extreme but because it's about an author whose work and life have profoundly influenced mine, involves Madeleine L'Engle, author of the young adult classic, *A Wrinkle in Time*.

L'Engle received two years' worth of rejections from twenty-six publishers for *A Wrinkle in Time*, which once it was finally published in 1962, went on to win major awards and be translated into more than a dozen languages. It was later adapted as both a miniseries and a feature film.

L'Engle's story is hardly unique. Here's a selection of other infamous rejections, beginning with the film world...

- Rejected by most Hollywood studios ("the worst thing ever written," according to a Columbia TriStar executive), *Pulp Fiction* went on to win the Palme d'Or at Cannes and a best screen-writing Oscar for Roger Avery and Quentin Tarantino.

- Dropping Stephen Spielberg into the director's chair didn't initially help *Raiders of the Lost Ark*, which most studios considered too expensive for a film with no big-name stars attached. *Raiders of the Lost Ark* won five of its nine Oscar nominations and is now considered to be one of the best action-adventure films of all time.

- It took some forty-four rejections before Universal said yes to *Back to the Future*. Other studios had complained that it was either "too family friendly" or "not family friendly enough." Disney was alarmed by allusions to mother-son incest, while Columbia felt it was "not sexual enough." *Back to the Future* was nominated for

234 MARK DAVID GERSON

more than two dozen awards, including four Oscars (it won one) and four Golden Globes. It was the top-grossing film in 1985.

From the literary world...

- J.K. Rowling was rejected by a dozen publishers before Bloomsbury embraced the first Harry Potter novel and only, legend has it, because the CEO's eight-year-old daughter insisted. Rowling and her books have gone on to make literary and film history.

- Theodore Geisel's first book as Dr. Seuss was turned down twenty-seven times before landing a publishing contract. Geisel ultimately won two Oscars and two Emmys, as well as the Pulitzer Prize and a Peabody Award.

- Jack Canfield and Mark Victor Hansen had both J.K. Rowling and Dr. Seuss beat: The original *Chicken Soup for the Soul* book was rejected by more than a hundred publishers ("nobody wants to read a book of short little stories") before it launched a multimillion-dollar franchise.

- Publishing giant Alfred A. Knopf rejected Jack Kerouac's *On the Road*, dismissing it as a huge, sprawling and inconclusive novel that would attract small sales and garner indignant reviews. Knopf also rejected George Orwell's *Animal Farm* ("it is impossible to sell animal stories in the U.S.A."), as well as Sylvia Plath ("there certainly isn't enough genuine talent for us to take notice"), Anne Frank, Isaac Bashevis Singer ("it's Poland and the rich Jews again") and Vladimir Nabokov.

- Kurt Vonnegut, William Faulkner, Judy Blume, Jorge Luis Borges ("utterly untranslatable"), Norman Mailer ("this will set publishing back twenty-five years"), James Joyce and D.H. Lawrence also received multiple rejections before finally getting a yes.

- Other literary rebuffs? William Golding's *Lord of the Flies*, Oscar Wilde's *Lady Windemere's Fan*, Joseph Heller's *Catch-22*, Anita Loos's *Gentlemen Prefer Blondes*, John le Carré's *The Spy Who Came in from the Cold* ("you're welcome to le Carré — he hasn't got any future"), Stephen King's *Carrie* (rejected thirty times), Kenneth Grahame's *The Wind in the Willows* ("an irresponsible holiday story"), the original "Tarzan of the Apes" story by Edgar Rice Burroughs, F. Scott Fitzgerald's *The Great Gatsby* ("you'd have a decent book if you'd get rid of that Gatsby character") and Gertrude Stein's *The Making of Americans* ("Only one look, only one look is enough. Hardly one copy would sell here. Hardly one. Hardly one").

And for fun, a pair of rejections of a different sort...

• On New Year's Day 1962, Decca executives in London auditioned a little-known rock 'n' roll band for a grueling two hours and fifteen songs. After a two-week, nail-biting wait, the band's manager finally heard back from Decca's Dick Rowe: "Not to mince words, Mr. Epstein," Rowe wrote, "but we don't like your boys' sound. Groups are out; four-piece groups with guitars particularly are finished." The manager was Brian Epstein. The group, of course, was The Beatles.

• William Orton, president of the Western Union Telegraph Company, turned away Alexander Graham Bell, calling his telephone an "electrical toy."

Toward the end of her demoralizing two-year period of rejections, Madeleine L'Engle covered up her typewriter and decided to give up — not only on *A Wrinkle in Time* but on writing. On her way to the kitchen, she had an epiphany: an idea for a novel about failure. In a flash, Madeleine L'Engle was back at her typewriter.

"That night," she explained three decades later in a PBS documentary, "I wrote in my journal, 'I'm a writer. That's who I am. That's what I am. That's what I have to do — even if I'm never, ever published again.' And I had to take seriously the fact that I might never, ever be published again. ... It's easy to say I'm a writer now, but I said it when it was hard to say. And I meant it."

ASK YOURSELF THESE QUESTIONS

• Can I refuse to let criticism or rejection stop me from moving forward with this screenplay or with any other of my writing projects?

• If an option or sale eludes me, can I trust that there may be other reasons why I was called to write this screenplay? Can I be okay with that?

Fade Out

MERYL STREEP (OSCAR-WINNING ACTOR)

You just have to keep your dream. If you lose it and get cynical, you die.

PRESTON STURGES (OSCAR-WINNING SCREENWRITER OF "THE GREAT MCGINTY")

When the last dime is gone, I'll sit on the curb outside with a pencil and a ten-cent notebook and start the whole thing over again.

Trust. Let Go. Leap.

Before he died, Apple's Steve Jobs said, "You have to trust in something — your gut, destiny, life, karma, whatever. This approach has never let me down, and it has made all the difference in my life."

That "something" has never let me down either. Over the years in both my writing and my life, I have taken many risks that defy logic and convention. And although I have experienced terror and discomfort along the way, the ultimate rewards have far outweighed the fallout.

I would still be living in Toronto right now had I ignored the 1997 call to hit the road I describe in "Surrender to the Journey" (Rule #2 for writing your screenplay). A similar if tenfold-longer odyssey in the decade that followed brought me to New Mexico and allowed me to gift myself and the world with, at this writing, three optioned screenplays and more than a dozen published books.

Through that time, I have discovered that once I commit to always following the highest possible path and purpose, a trinity of principles is consistently at play:

Trust. Let Go. Leap.

First, I trust the voice of my deepest heart, which is also the voice of my highest imperative and the voice of my Muse — the voice of what I sometimes call "infinite mind."

Next, I let go all resistance, all clinging and all clutching (which does not mean that I'm not afraid and which also does not mean that I have to know how whatever I'm being called to do is possible).

Finally, I leap into the void — just like the Fool does in most tarot decks.

I do it on the page, and I do it in my life.

Of course, I'm not always eager. "You want me to do *what* and go *where*?" I have been known to exclaim when presented with a next step, or with the next turn of a story's plot.

Yet once the initial shock dissipates, I surrender to the higher imperative: I trust, let go and leap...and watch everything begin to fall into place, often miraculously.

Miracles are present in every moment of our lives, including in our creative lives. It's our limited vision that prevents us from seeing them. It's our limited sense of what is possible that prevents us from believing in them. It's our fear that prevents us from embracing them.

Those miracles are available to us as magnificently in our writing as they are in our lives. What else would you call the logic-defying cohesion of *The Legend of Q'ntana*, each of its stories written with little or no conscious notion of its plot, except as its words moved through me onto the page?

Trust.

Let Go.

Leap.

In my writing as in my life, it always works.

TRY THIS

Writing is an act of pilgrimage. We set out on a journey, often intent on a particular direction and destination. Yet if we are true to our art and true to our heart, we free the story to carry us where it will. The resulting journey is one that reveals to us not only the story we are writing but the story we are living.

When we listen for the stories that move through us, we also discover the story that is us.

How has your writing been a pilgrimage? What has it taught you — about yourself, about your work, about the world? Write about that without thinking too deeply about it. Instead, let the Muse Stream reveal to you what you didn't know you knew.

It's Time to Live the Dream

What is your dream for your writing? Know that whatever it is, however improbable it may seem in this moment, it is not impossible.

Nearly every success story begins with an "impossible" dream. Nearly every "overnight success" was years in the making.

So, what about *your* dreams? Have you abandoned them? Stuffed them in the back of a drawer because they seemed so unreachable?

Open that drawer. Reach your hand in. Gently. Touch it. Reconnect with it. Reconnect with yourself.

Have you begun the screenplay that was the reason you came to this book?

If not, then now is the time to put your dream into action. It doesn't matter whether you can give it five minutes a day or five hours. It doesn't even matter whether you know in this moment what it's about or where it will take you.

Every journey begins with a single step. Every piece of writing begins with a single word. One word. Any word.

Write that word. Now.

Open your heart again. Open your heart to the vision. Open your heart to yourself. Open your heart to your life. Say yes to you. Say yes to the screenwriter you are!

TRY THIS

Write on the Muse Stream from the phrase "I am ready to live my dream..." If you know what your dreams are, let this be a statement of commitment and part of your first step in realizing them. If you don't, let yourself discover dreams you never knew you had through this writing exploration.

TRY THIS TOO

If you have yet to begin your screenplay, now is the time to launch into it. Don't think about what you're going to write. Don't try to figure out anything about it. Just start. Write now!

You Are A Writer:
A Guided Meditation

I include this meditation in all my books for writers because it is too easy, as creative artists working largely in isolation, to diminish both ourselves and our output and to forget that we are powerful and empowered creators.

Listen to this meditation when you feel doubt...when you feel less-than...when you don't believe that you will ever be able to complete your screenplay...when you question whether you are even a writer.

In those moments, let the words and spirit of this meditation remind you that you are a writer of power, passion, strength and courage. For writing is an act of courage... of immeasurable courage. And you are doing it!

Allow 5 minutes for this meditative experience.

A professionally recorded meditation similar to this one is available for download or streaming.[1] See "Getting Started" (Scene 1) for details on how to access the recording, as well as for tips on how best to use this book's meditations.

Close your eyes and take a few deep breaths as you relax and listen...

You are a writer. You are a writer of power, passion, strength and, yes, courage. For writing is an act of courage. Acknowledge that courage, the courage that got you to this point...having written. Having written today, if you have. Having written just now, if you have.

You are a writer. Breathe in to that. Breathe in to the release you felt as the pen flowed across the page, as letters formed into words, words stretched into sentences and sentences began to fill your pages.

Breathe in to the freedom, the vibrancy, the love. Breathe in to the

---

[1] Search the relevant site/store for "Mark David Gerson you are a writer"

knowledge and knowingness that you can do it again. And again. And again. And again.

You are a writer. What you write is powerful. What you write is vibrant. What you write, whatever you believe in this moment, is luminous.

Trust that to the best of your ability, in this moment. Acknowledge the writer you are, in this moment. Breathe in to that.

Breathe out judgment. Breathe out fear. Breathe out not-good-enoughs. Breathe out comparisons. What others have written does not matter. What you have written is all that matters now, in this moment. It is perfect...in this moment. Know that. Trust that. Breathe in to that.

If you don't feel ready to read what you have written from that place of trust, discernment and compassion, set it aside. Set it aside for a time — until you arrive at a place of more clarity, more objectivity, more self-love.

Don't avoid reading it, but nor do you need to rush into it. Either way, for now know that you are a writer. A writer writes. That's what you have done. You have written.

You are a **writer.**

You **are** a writer.

You are a writer.

You have heard the words. Now speak them with me...

I am a **writer.**

I **am** a writer.

I am a writer.

Speak them again and again and again, knowing them to be true. Speak them again, feeling the truth in them. Speak them again, for they are true.

Roll the Credits

My initial expression of gratitude goes not to a person but to a story: Without *The MoonQuest*, which urged itself on me in the midst of a writing class I was teaching more than twenty-five years ago, much of the creative richness I have experienced in the years since would not have been possible. Without *The MoonQuest* book, there would have been no *Legend of Q'ntana* screenplays and without *The Legend of Q'ntana* screenplays, there could have been no *Organic Screenwriting*.

Given that, my first "human" thanks goes to my first mentor, Carole H. Leckner, who kept asking me to teach until I finally said yes and whose gentle but firm encouragement helped me dismantle my many writing blocks.

If Carole started me teaching, the many hundreds of writers I have been privileged to touch over the years — in classes, workshops and talks, and as coach and mentor — have kept me teaching. Thank you all for reminding me, again and again, how galvanizing and inspiring my words, tools and techniques can be and for believing in me even in those moments when I'm challenged to believe in myself. Thanks, too, to my even more numerous online friends and followers for always cheering me on — never more so than on this book. And a particular shout-out to the many screenwriters whose enthusiastic response to my organic approach to the craft urged me to put it into a book.

I must also single out Aalia Golden, the friend who badgered me into adapting *The MoonQuest* for the screen, and film producer Kathleen Messmer, who not only loved the resulting script but urged me to craft film versions of *The StarQuest* and *The SunQuest*, two other of my *Q'ntana* novels, and to write this book. Kathleen is also a gifted photographer and I owe her a debt of gratitude for this edition's cover image.

Over the years, I have crafted chunks of many of my writing projects in cafes, and *Organic Screenwriting* was no different. To the baristas of the half-dozen Albuquerque Starbucks outlets where this book was conceived and birthed, I was the bearded, anxious-looking, caffeine-infused, black-clad guy huddled over his laptop who kept ordering Americanos topped with extra-hot steamed 2%. Thank you for your forbearance!

Finally, as always, to my Muse: I thought my *Acts of Surrender* memoir was the book I didn't want to write. I was wrong. *This* was the book I didn't want to write! That you kept at me until I surrendered and then kept at me some more until I finished is a gift whose value I am still experiencing, a gift that is beyond measure. Thank you.

Made in the USA
Monee, IL
19 January 2024

52072674R00143